Mel Bay Presents

INTERVIEWS WITH THE JAZZ GREATS

...AND MORE

BY CHARLES CHAPMAN

Visit us on the Web at www.melbay.com — E-mail us at email@melbay.com

Foreword

As a free-lance music journalist, one of my favorite assignments is conducting artist interviews. Since my background is that of a jazz guitarist, most of the assignments have been in that specific genre. To my delight I have occasionally been asked to stray from my roots and chat with interesting artists in the contemporary rock arena and in 1996 interviewed the renowned luthier Robert Benedetto.

Putting this montage together for Mel Bay Publications, Inc. brought back a flood of pleasant memories. It is truly the first time I have looked at this body of work as one identity and was amazed at the many threads that weaved through these great artists. The passion for their art, the sense of sharing and passing on to the next generation is immediately apparent. All in all, a true love of the guitar and music is always evident.

These interviews were all assignments and the length has absolutely nothing to do with my personal feelings about the artist or their legacy. In most cases a word count was strictly enforced making it necessary to hone the verbiage to the bare bones. In retrospect, this may be good as it provides a pleasant read and overview of just a few of the greats that you may or may not have been aware of.

Hopefully in years to come a second volume will be possible. The music, the artists and their instruments, are a large part of my life and I would love to continue to share the words of wisdom from the living legends to the young lions of this wonderful instrument we call the guitar.

Special thanks to Ed Benson (*Just Jazz Guitar* magazine), Ron Bentley (Berklee College of Music), Stephen Rekas (Mel Bay Publications) and Donna Chapman (photography). Without their support this project would never have come to fruition.

Table of Contents

Article on 7-String guitar with quotes from George Van Eps,
Bucky Pizzarelli, Howard Alden, Steve Vai, Fred Fried and luthiers Bob Benedetto and Bill Conklin

John Abercrombie – (November 1995)

John Abercrombie grew up in Greenwich, Connecticut and in 1962 enrolled in, what was then, Berklee School of Music. Since Berklee, Abercrombie has pushed the musical boundaries while maintaining a connection to the traditional formats which triggered his interest in jazz. He performed in the early jazz-rock group Dreams, fusion with Billy Cobham, free-jazz with Jack DeJohnette and classical and world-rooted jazz with Ralph Towner. He has also performed with John Scofield, Bill Evans, George Mraz, McCoy Tyner, Michael Brecker and Jan Hammer. John is an ECM recording artist with literally dozens of albums in his catalog. He and his group recently returned from a very successful tour of Hungary, Turkey, Germany, Yugoslavia and Italy.

The following interview was conducted at John's home in Manhattan on November 8, 1995.

Charles Chapman: Guitarists in general, specifically those who graduate from Berklee, often migrate to NYC to fulfill their musical aspirations. They often consult you to help them refine their playing. Are there any areas in which you find they are consistently lacking?

John Abercrombie: The most problematic area for all guitarists is their rhythm. Most of my students know their scales better than I do. A few years ago that was not the case. I try to get my students centered in the rhythm of what they're playing and try to hear and feel instead of just whipping around the fretboard. Many times students get so obsessed with the fretboard they forget they're playing with a band. They then become a guitarist and not a musician. Guitar students, in all styles, try to play too many notes.

Students will often ask me to show them how to improvise over changes in a more modern way. They're usually shocked to find I don't have a modern approach. I'm not trying to be modern—I'm just trying to make the changes and play what I hear.

CC: You've stated many times that Jim Hall and Bill Evans were your two main inspirations. Could you elaborate on that?

JA: I originally heard Jim Hall with the Art Farmer Quartet in the mid 1960s. It was the group where Steve Swallow was still playing upright bass. What struck me the most about Jim was not only the way he soloed, but how he worked with a band. He didn't just play traditional guitar voicings. He had clustered voicings, voicings in 4ths, and would play guide tones and counterpoint to the soloist or behind the melody. Jim could fit in with modern players and never sound old fashioned. Up to this point in time guitarists generally didn't play like this. When I heard Jim Hall it was instantaneous, this was how I wanted to play.

Before Jim, Wes Montgomery was my role model and still is in certain ways. Jim's harmonic sense is so developed that it always amazes me. About a year ago I had the privilege of performing with Jim in Missouri and he kicked my butt all over the stage and sounded a hell of a lot more modern than I did. He never plays fast just for the sake of playing fast—he plays intervals, melodies and thematic ideas. Initially Bill Evans intrigued me with his group interplay. Especially in his trio's—the one that comes to mind is with Scott LaFaro and Paul Motian. His harmonic sense was truly unbelievable. His reharmonizations were impeccable. Even when I hear the original version of a tune it's Bill's reharm that I always like the best. Like Jim, Bill's music moves me—there is a real emotional aspect to it. It wasn't just like: WOW listen to the pretty chords.

Bass and drums just didn't mark time in Bill's groups, there was a dialog between the soloist and the group. When Bill and Jim performed together it made total sense and demonstrated the way music should be played.

CC: Within the last two years it seems like you've abandoned the pick...

JA: No, not totally. In fact, I was using a pick last night because I needed to dig in a little more. Over the last few years I've migrated towards using my thumb as sort of a replacement for the pick. For me it's perfect because I was never one to play a lot of fast lines so using my thumb gives me a warmer sound and it really doesn't hurt my technique. I may have lost a little speed, but not enough to worry about. I still keep my pick tucked away in my hand or near by. I'm never far from it because there are times when I need it to give me that added edge. I use it more sonically than for speed purposes.

CC: What do you consider your main guitars and what is your basic equipment setup?

JA: The electric guitar I use predominantly is made by Roger Sadowsky and is similar to a Telecaster style instrument. The humbucker is in the front position, a single coil in the middle, and another humbucker in the bridge position. I also play an Ibanez solid body Artist model and a Chet Atkins steel string.

My equipment setup consists of a Stewart preamp for the Chet Atkins and a Walter Woods power amp. For effects I use a Boss SE 50. It's a really cheap multi-effects unit, but I like the way it sounds.

CC: Do you think you will ever get back into the guitar synthesizer?

JA: I doubt it. I gave away all my equipment to my brother-in-law. The only thing I kept was the GR 300 which is the one Pat Metheny uses. The unit and the guitar have been sitting in a corner of my studio for a very long time, I don't think I've even turned it on in years.

CC: You stated in a *Downbeat* magazine interview that the guitar synth bores you. Could you elaborate?

JA: There's nothing wrong with the guitar synth, but for me I became obsessed with the sounds. You keep looking for more cards and waiting in anticipation for new updates to come out. In reality I discovered it was the basic guitar sounds that intrigued me. I went back to basic guitar and effects and I've been happy ever since. I have to admit that in the beginning stages the synth was great for me. It made me delve into music in a different way. It inspired me to do a lot of writing, but then it was time to return to what I loved. I just got tired of the technology and wanted to create music.

CC: Could you comment on any upcoming projects?

JA: My current trio, with Dan Wall on Hammond organ and Adam Nissbaum on drums, made a live recording in July at Visioni's here in the city and it's suppose to be out by summer '96.

CC: What advice could you give a guitar student preparing for a career in music?

JA: Try all possibilities, delve into jazz and improvisation. Learn all about rock styles and try to experience all you can about music to get a good overall picture of the possibilities. Then trust your heart and go in your own direction. Don't listen to your brain too much. If you want to be an artist— listen to your heart.

Photo by Donna Chapman

John and Charles at the CA. NAMM Show

Howard Alden — (December 1999)

Howard Alden is one of a handful of up-and-coming guitarists bringing the seven-string archtop to the forefront of jazz. His prowess as a single string improviser is daunting and his insight into fretboard harmony and chord construction is second to none.

Born in Newport Beach, California in 1958, Alden began playing guitar and tenor banjo as a child. Alden's early influences were Louis Armstrong, Barney Kessel, and Charlie Christian and later developed a passion for the harmonies and textures of music by Bill Evans and Thelonious Monk. He moved to New York in 1982 where he still resides.

Alden was voted "Best Emerging Guitar Talent" in the first annul *Jazztimes* critics poll in 1990 and "Talent Deserving Wider Recognition" in the '92, '93, '95, and '96 *Downbeat* critics polls. In November '97 opened the world famous Chinery Exhibition at the Smithsonian Institution's Museum of American History. He continues to challenge his creativity by performing in different instrumental combinations and settings.

To quote the master luthier Robert Benedetto:

"No doubt if you looked up Howard Alden in Webster's dictionary, he would be defined as "The Consummate Guitarist." Howard doesn't hold the guitar as he plays—he caresses it. As if being a world-class player isn't enough, he is also one of the most decent human beings I've ever had the pleasure of calling a friend. I'm at a loss for words when trying to describe Howard's playing style. He does everything with impeccable taste and truly plays as if the guitar were just another appendage. In another life, he must have been a guitar!"

The following interview was conducted at Howard's home in New York City on December 5, 1999.

Charles Chapman: Who or what events initially inspired you to play guitar?

Howard Alden: Believe or not, I first became interested in guitar through TV shows like *Hee Haw*. I used to see these guys playing guitar and having such great fun. What really sold me on jazz guitar was when I heard a record by Barney Kessel. I just loved the sound and his whole approach. I loved the way he combined chords and single notes, the swing and the way he developed his ideas just fascinated me. My first instrument was the tenor banjo and I was first introduced to jazz by Jim Elsaas, who was a part time tenor banjo and guitar player. He had a great collection of all the classic jazz records and he was kind enough to share them with me. He had records by all the great jazz guitarists: Barney, Kenny Burrel, Charlie Christian, Tal Farlow, Django Reinhardt, etc. but it was those Kessel records that really hooked me.

CC: How old were you when you began to play an instrument and was music a part of your household growing up?

HA: When I was about ten years old, I found a four-string guitar and a tenor banjo in a closet. The banjo was an old Vega Little Wonder—a tiny 17-fret model. The guitar was a Regal flat-top with a very small body—only a little larger than a baritone uke. I was self taught and played just for the enjoyment of it. I was around 12 when I seriously started to take an interest in guitar and jazz. My family liked music and growing up there was always music playing from show tunes, popular music and a little jazz, but they were not professional musicians or anything like that.

CC: You have an extensive repertoire. How do you go about learning tunes and do you have trouble retaining them?

HA: Good question. I've always learned a lot of tunes from my early days on banjo and then on the guitar. Learning tunes was always a part of my daily practice routine, much more than scales or other technical elements of music. I'm blessed with a good memory and now it's gotten to the point that if I've heard something I can play it. As long as I can hear the tune in my head I can get it out on the guitar. Most tunes are based on basic dance band harmony and I have most of those progressions locked in my head, so it's not that hard or all that unusual.

CC: Are you currently involved in teaching as well as performing and recording?

HA: Just a little. When I was in my teens I went to GIT (Guitar Institute of Technology) in Hollywood right after Howard Roberts became involved with it. After being a student I stayed on as an assistant and then became an instructor. After a few years I really became burned out with teaching and dealing with so many guitar players. That is when I decided to put all my efforts into performing and moved to New York City. I still occasionally teach a few private students or present a clinic, but it's rare. My performing schedule is so inconsistent and I do so much traveling that teaching is not really practical at this stage of my career.

CC: What's the story on the Woody Allen movie that you've been involved with?

HA: The movie officially opened this week and I saw it for the first time last Tuesday. The movie is titled *Sweet and Lowdown* and it is a Woody Allen movie that he wrote and directed. It is about a fictitious jazz guitar player in the 1930s and is not about Django even though his name is mentioned throughout the movie. The main character's name is Emmett Ray (played by Sean Penn) and it's built up around dramatic and humorous vignettes around this guy and features a lot of guitar playing. I played all the lead and solo parts with the great jazz guitarist Bucky Pizzarelli playing rhythm—

which was a tremendous honor and thrill for me. There were quite a few solo and duo guitar tracks, but the film soundtrack also features Ken Peplowski on clarinet, Kelly Friesen on bass and Ted Somer on drums. Sean Penn played the lead and a very talented English actress, Samantha Morton was also featured. She plays a mute and doesn't speak, but her facial expressions and body language were just incredible. Also featured were actors James Urbaniak, Uma Thurman and the Music Director was Dick Hyman. Woody Allen not only directed, but researched the history, and picked the music. He was great to work with.

CC: What was your affiliation with Sean Penn and is he a guitarist?

HA: Dick Hyman approached me about this film approximately two years ago. He wanted to know if I could record a few tunes in the style of Django Reinhardt with only about two days of studio time. An appointment was set up for me to meet the producer, I played a few tunes and before I knew it he asked if I would be interested in being Sean Penn's guitar coach. The job changed from being two days in the studio to six months of work. I was on the set almost every day which was mostly filmed all around NY city, but briefly traveled to San Francisco and Italy to work with Sean.

CC: What was it like to work with Sean Penn?

HA: He was the consummate professional. He was a hard worker and very easy to get along with, a very serious guy who was also very down to earth. He had no prior experience with guitar or jazz, but got right into it and started practicing. By the time we finished he could play a few tunes, but was basically miming the parts I played. He picked up extremely quick and was very astute. In fact, he picked up on my movements and a lot of things I never realized I did. After about a month working with him he used to joke and say: "Who wants to see my Howard Alden impression?"

CC: Tell us about how you initially met George Van Eps and your relationship with him?

HA: The first time I met George was right before I moved to NY in the early 80s. He had just come out of retirement and had finished the (Mel Bay Publications) book series, "Harmonic Mechanisms for Guitar" and was promoting it at the NAMM show in California. I was in such awe that all I could do was shake his hand and mumble a little. The second time was a few years later at a jazz festival in western Pennsylvania. I was playing at the show and George was booked with a band that was sort of a recreation of the historic Pete Kelly's Blues Band—mostly studio players from LA. I got to know him a little and he came to hear me play; I did one of his solos that he seemed to like. We hit it off very well and I was ecstatic. A couple of years later I was booked at a Labor Day jazz festival in Los Angeles and somehow was teamed up to play a couple of sets with him. It went well and I was honored to have actually performed with Mr. Van Eps, but really didn't give it any more thought. On one of my first albums for Concord Records I played a Van Eps solo arrangement, and mentioned in the liner notes how I had previously performed with him and was one of the thrills of my life. Carl Jefferson who was president of Concord Records called me and stated that he thought we should do an album together. That possibility never crossed my mine. One thing lead to another and we made the album.

CC: How many albums did you do with George and did you do any live concerts, etc.?

HA: We collaborated on four albums and I managed to get him on a few brief tours with me. We went to Europe, England and also played a few dates in the United States.

CC: Over the years you have amply demonstrated your prowess over the Van Eps solo repertoire, but you seem to favor two Van Eps solos: *48* and *Tango El Bongo*. Is there a story here?

HA: Not really. I like both these tunes very much and for some reason I can always keep these two particular pieces under my fingers. I feel very comfortable with those arrangements and often include them in my solo sets.

CC: The album *The Concord Jazz Collective* with guitarists Jimmy Bruno and Frank Vignola was a critically acclaimed album. Do you have any plans to do a *Collective II* recording?

HA: I would really like to do that because playing with Jimmy and Frank is always a treat. We have a live recording that we've talked about releasing, but haven't done anything as yet. Jimmy and Frank bring out different aspects of my playing and they

are very exciting to perform with. They both have such incredibly quick ears.

CC: Was it George Van Eps who inspired you to switch to the 7-string guitar?

HA: A combination of Van Eps and being around Bucky Pizzarelli. Bucky is so outgoing and friendly that whenever we would meet he would let me mess around with his guitar. I always shied away from it, but he was extremely encouraging. In fact, while Bob Benedetto was making my first 7-string, Bucky loaned me one of his to practice on. Finally, sitting down next to George when we made our first album did it for me. Sitting next to him and seeing what he could do, that was when I knew I had to get into the 7-string guitar.

CC: Would you recommend a student start on the 7-string?

HA: Sure, why not. With the 7-string guitar everything is right there and the fact that you have that seventh string means your harmony is more complete—you're still only playing two or three notes at a time.

CC: The last time we spoke you had just taken possession of a 7-string acoustic Benedetto La Venezia model. You are now playing another very unique Benedetto model, what is it?

HA: Bob and I designed a smaller model that is just great. It is 14 and half inches wide with a 2 and a quarter inch body depth. It has a custom shaped sound opening with one built in Benedetto B-7 pickup with a push/pull volume and tone knobs. It's very different from my other guitars and I love it. In fact, a 6-string version of this Bob calls the "Bambino" will be unveiled at NAMM this year as one of the Benedetto models Guild will be displaying.

CC: What other guitars do you own?

HA: I own three other Benedetto 7-strings that are great and I really have no desire to play anything else.

CC: Give us a brief rundown on how they differ?

HA: My first 7-string Bob made for me was a 16-inch archtop with an oval soundhole. The second is similar, but with a unique fan bracing pattern. I don't understand a lot about the finer points, but both are tremendous and are fitted with custom Benedetto suspended pickups. My third guitar is a Benedetto La Venezia 7-string. The LaVenezia is a 17 inch, has f sound holes and is a completely acoustic archtop with no pickup. This has a gorgeous sound! In fact, Bucky liked it so much that he used it for just about all the rhythm tracks on *Sweet and Lowdown.* I was beginning to get a little scared that he wasn't going to give it back.

CC: Give us the rundown on the rest of your gear?

HA: I endorse Polytone amps and recently have been using the "Mega Brute" that only has an eight inch speaker. It's small, light and great to use around New York City. I can't believe how good the bass response is and it has more than enough power for what I do. I use GHS strings for all my guitars: Gauges .013, .017, .024, .036, .046, .056, and .080 for the seventh. The exception is the La Venezia where I use GHS Vintage Bronze. Gauges are the same except the sixth string is a .058 and I also use .080 on the seventh.

CC: Have you explored guitar technology, pedals, effects, MIDI, etc.?

HA: For the last few years I have been doing a lot of my music on computer, but as yet have not gotten into MIDI or other technologies. I am not opposed to any kind of sound enhancement or new innovations, and may someday explore the benefits, but it's not a priority at the moment.

CC: Advice to beginning guitarists?

HA: Develop your repertoire. You're better off spending time learning and practicing tunes rather than running scales up and down the neck. Play with other people as much as possible. An hour spent playing with other musicians is worth six hours practicing by yourself.

CC: Any upcoming projects you could share with us?

HA: I have a solo album in the can. I just have to get around to putting it together and it should be out on the Concord label in the next few months. Next March, I will be on a six week tour. It's called the "Newport Millennium Tour—A Hundred Years of Jazz" and is sponsored by the people that put on the

Newport Jazz Festival (Festival Productions). It will go from March 1st through April 8th and will be all one nighters across the country. I'm the only guitarist and will feature Nickolous Payton and Randy Brecker on trumpets, Joel Helleny, a wonderful trombone player, Lew Tabackin and a host of others. There will be ten or twelve musicians in all and it sounds like great fun.

Photo by Donna Chapman

Howard, Charles and Bob Benedetto at the Classic American Guitar Show, NY.

Photo by Donna Chapman

Howard Alden at a NAMM show concert

Robert Benedetto – *(December 1996)*

In the highly selective world of mainstream jazz, the instrument of choice has historically been the archtop guitar. From Charlie Christian and Wes Montgomery to the young lions of the jazz world today, the archtop still remains supreme. This eclectic instrument is distinctly American. The first carved-top guitar was designed by Orville Gibson in the late 1800s when he applied European violin making techniques to steel string guitars and mandolins. In the 20th Century John D'Angelico attained the title "The Stradivarius of Guitar Makers" when he took the craft of making an archtop guitar to an art form. He died on September 1, 1964 at the young age of 59 —leaving the throne vacant. Since that time there have been numerous archtop makers achieving critical acclaim, but none so much as Robert Benedetto. When speaking with jazz guitarists to collectors on who should be the rightful heir—the name Benedetto consistently emerges.

Bob was born in the Bronx, New York in 1946 and came from three generations of woodworkers, artists and musicians. By age 13 he was playing guitar professionally in local bands, already starting to develop a sense of what he wanted in an instrument. In his early guitar-making years, he also did many repairs and restorations thus enabling him to study the inner workings of fine instruments like D'Angelicos, Strombergs, Gibsons and Epiphones. Bob's reputation grew as he started to make instruments for many of the better guitarists in New York City and elsewhere. For three decades, Benedetto instruments have been played by many of the top jazz musicians and are renowned worldwide for their tonal balance, ease of playing and highly cultivated sense of style. Guitarists such as Chuck Wayne, Johnny Smith, Bucky Pizzarelli, Howard Alden, Jimmy Bruno and Andy Summers are just a few who own and play his instruments. Bob is also a skilled violin maker as well having made an instrument for the jazz violinist extraordinaire, Stephane Grappelle. Bob is one of a handful of builders who from the very beginning focused solely on the jazz guitar and its players. Highly innovative, over the course of his 30-year career he has acquired an unrivaled depth of understanding of the archtop guitar. Let's explore the intricate process of making an archtop as well as hearing from the man himself.

Charles Chapman: What initially led you to guitarmaking?

Robert Benedetto: As far back as I can remember, it's all I ever wanted to do. But not just any guitar—only the archtop.

CC: Did you ever make semi-acoustics or solid body instruments? If so, why do you not make them any more?

RB: I have made a variety of electrics over the years. I made six unusual semi-hollow bodies from 1982-1986 and about 200 solid body guitars and basses (at one point with John Buscarino) from 1986-1987. While they sold well, my main focus is still the full-bodied archtop.

CC: You also make a full line of "Benedetto" pickups. Do you wind them yourself? Tell us how they differ from the norm?

RB: My pickups are made to my specifications by Kent Armstrong in the UK (*editors note:* now being marketed by Seymour Duncan). They differ from others in that they are truly made for *jazz guitar*— fat, warm high end without the usual muddy lows. Perfectly balanced.

CC: You were the first guitar maker to use a cello tail adjuster to fasten the ebony tailpiece to the guitar. Exactly what is a cello tail adjuster and why do you use it?

RB: The cello tail adjuster loops around an end pin or end pin jack in order to attach the tailpiece to the body. It's the same material used on virtually every cello in the world today. It replaced real gut because it lasts forever. My tailpiece arrangement is very pure and eliminates metal brackets which dampen the guitar's acoustics.

CC: You are also the originator of the "ebonized" bridge adjuster wheels. Please explain what these are and how are they unique?

RB: The ebonized bridge adjusters are simply black height adjustment wheels. Just a cosmetic touch. The black wheels blend with the black ebony bridge which is pleasing to my eye.

CC: Why do you use an ebony nut instead of commonly used bone ones?

RB: Actually, I only use an ebony nut on guitars that have no binding. If a white bone nut is used on a guitar with no matching white binding on the neck or headstock, the white nut clashes. It breaks the continuity and visually "cuts off" the headstock. With traditional white binding, the white nut blends well.

CC: Your 7-String guitars are very popular. Did you start making them mainly on request or is this guitar one of your mainstay instruments?

RB: Both, I guess. The popularity of the 7-String guitar has been growing steadily for several years. It accounts for about 25% of my orders. Certainly players like Bucky Pizzarelli have encouraged others to play it. Although it's not for everyone, it certainly is here to stay. The additional bass string adds a whole new dimension to the player's thinking and playing.

CC: You are known as the master of restraint when it comes to guitar adornments. Other guitarmakers often use an incredible amount of inlay, fancy bindings, gold tuning pegs, etc.—your guitars are very straight forward. Please tell us about your esthetic principles.

RB: Actually, on my earlier guitars I did more inlay work than I do now, and even use to hand carve ornamentation on the rear of the headstocks. My customers liked that and it was difficult to convince them that without the unnecessary bindings and inlays, the guitar would sound better. Now, the unadorned guitars are finally more acceptable. Frequently, however, I do a delicate abalone inlay on the 12th fret — I think it's a classy touch and has become a trademark on my guitars.

CC: How many guitars have you made over the last three decades?

RB: I've made over 650 musical instruments to date, including 400 archtop guitars and over 200 solid bodies. I've also made 45 violins, 5 violas and have a cello in the works!

CC: How many guitars do you make in a year?

RB: About 30 archtops.

CC: What is the delivery time from when the initial deposit is given?

RB: 2½ — 3 years.

CC: If you were forced to name your favorite guitar, of all the ones you ever made, which one would it be?

RB: Truly, it would be impossible for me to answer that. Regardless of the model or price, some were good, some not so good and some were exceptional. I will say, for the past 10 years or so my instruments have been very consistent and I'm happy with what I hear.

CC: What led you to write the book, *Making an Archtop Guitar*, and film the instructional video, *Archtop Guitar Design & Construction*?

RB: Cindy! She has been supportive in every conceivable way and convinced me that with the archtop's growing popularity, I should write a book. So I did! It was Ed Benson's (editor of *Just Jazz Guitar* magazine) brainstorm to video one of my archtop guitarmaking classes since he was attending anyway. Another great idea!

GS: Tell us a little about the courses you taught on guitarmaking.

RB: A novel idea at the time, I taught my first course in the fall of 1992. It was a tremendous success and drew attendees from as far away as Australia. Classes varied from three days to one week. Amateurs to professionals signed up. I had to discontinue them because of time constraints, but I must say it's amazing how many people want to learn how to make a guitar. I still get calls.

CC: What are your thoughts on the future of the archtop guitar and what new directions do you see it heading?

RB: I don't think anybody is going to pull a rabbit out of a hat. The archtop has been a slowly evolving design, and that's probably the way things will continue. It's still a jazz guitar, so from a player's point of view it should feel, look and sound a certain way. If we deviate too much from that format it becomes a different instrument. Really, it all comes down to the player. It's the player's needs which will guide the maker.

Photo by Jonathan Levin

Bob buffing a back.

Bob carving a top.

Photo by Donna Chapman

Bob Benedetto and Charles with Bob's one-of-a-kind solid body creation "The Pizzar Guitar".

14

Benedetto/Guild Interview – *(May 1999)*

In November of 1995, two decades of managerial ups and downs ended when Fender Musical Instruments purchased Guild from the US Music Corporation. Under new leadership, Guild's original pursuit of quality gained new energy—new processes and controls were introduced, new equipment was purchased and, most importantly, the new management brought a level of commitment to quality not seen at Guild since Al Dronge (original founder and President of Guild).

On March 10, 1999 Guild took its commitment to quality one step further by signing a "Design and Consultant Agreement" with the world-renowned archtop jazz builder Bob Benedetto.

Bob has agreed to work with Guild's factory at Westerly, Rhode Island to enhance the quality of Guild's flagship Artist Award and Stuart model jazz guitars. The Guild Custom Shop in Nashville will also benefit from Benedetto's expertise and will become the builders of a select number of Benedetto models. This is definitely a win win situation for everyone—especially the guitarist of tomorrow who will now be able to avail themselves of the artistry that only so few could in the past.

Charles Chapman: Why would the world's most successful archtop maker want to become involved with a major guitar manufacturer?

Bob Benedetto: It's the dream of every individual guitar maker to want to expand his horizons, to have his name and work go further than just one person can do alone. Joining forces with a respected large manufacturer fulfills that dream, to the benefit of both parties. But truthfully, I wouldn't do it with just any manufacturer. I've always had a great deal of respect for Guild.

CC: Why did you specifically want your name associated with Guild?

BB: Guild is the perfect company for me to be associated with. They always made wonderful instruments. Years ago during my repair days, I would often have one on the bench and thought, "If I could only get into that factory, I'd love to fine tune these guitars." Now, I'll have that opportunity

and the timing couldn't be better. The company has had its ups and downs for many years, but they held on. They have a very talented and dedicated staff. Plus, Guild and I have something in common—from the very beginning, we both started by making archtops. Now, with Fender behind Guild, there's nothing but a bright future for us all. I feel very safe knowing that Fender, with its long, successful history and revered image, is at the helm.

CC: How did this union come about?

BB: Good timing—that's everything. Fender obviously purchased Guild because they knew it was a good company, with lots of potential. One of the major objectives was to go further with the archtop line. With a little encouragement from one Charles Chapman (laughs), I received a call from Bill Acton last December. One word led to another and before I knew it we were working on a contract to not only update and improve the Artist Award and Stuart models, but also to make Benedettos at the Guild Custom Shop in Nashville.

CC: Excuse my impertinence, but many in the lutherie community may accuse you of "selling out" and only joining forces with Guild for monetary reasons. How will you respond to this?

BB: You may be surprised, but we've heard nothing but cheers from the lutherie community. By and large we individual makers, although competitive at times, are a very supportive group. We all know what it's like to struggle and share the same dream. And believe me, it's not only about money. It's much bigger than that. The reason I'm so excited about this arrangement is because I'm being given an opportunity to go further. With Guild's support, I'll be able to make my own line of guitars more accessible in the marketplace, plus I'll have time to do R&D work that's years overdue. There are so many things that could be done to improve the archtop guitar, and now I'll be able to do them, something I'd probably never have the time to do on my own.

CC: What is the impetus behind Guild's decision to have you upgrade the Artist Award and Stuart models?

BB: While Guild was aware that these two models were great guitars, they were also aware that they needed refining. I can remember the earliest years of the Artist Award. I even recall restoring one when it was called the Johnny Smith Award. They looked and felt right. Yet, over the years I watched and felt they were not advancing in the marketplace. The reason was obvious. While an occasional change in design was common enough, the guitars did not seem to be evolving. Fortunately, the workmanship at Guild has always been first-rate. That makes my job much easier. The Guild staff is already a fine group of dedicated artisans. I'm just going to help them fine tune these already great instruments.

CC: I understand a number of the existing Benedetto standard models will now be available exclusively through Guild's Nashville Custom Shop.

BB: Yes. Most of the popular models, like the Manhattan, the "Benny" and a few others, are now going to be made there under my supervision. I'll also continue making guitars at my own shop, but only one-of-a-kind custom instruments.

CC: On most high end archtops, spruce is used for the top and maple for the back, sides and neck. I know you have built a few instruments with rosewood, mahogany, etc. Do you have any plans of experimenting with alternate wood sources for future projects with Guild or on your own?

BB: Alternate woods are one of the things I hope to address. There's no doubt about traditional maple and spruce being the best choice on the traditional archtop. There are, however, a lot of new instrument designs bouncing around in my head. A completely new archtop design is where alternative woods would be a really good consideration.

CC: Could you give us your opinion on built-in versus floating style pickups on carved archtops?

BB: It really is a matter of personal preference. One is not necessarily better than the other. It just depends on what each individual player prefers. I've made several finely tuned acoustic archtops with one built-in pickup, and I'm usually surprised how good these guitars sound acoustically.

CC: You are well known for your 7-String archtop. Will that model also be offered at the Custom Shop?

BB: Sure! The Custom Shop is a small group of really fine guitarmakers. They cater to the niche market, something the large factories are not set up to do.

CC: Besides the fact that Robert Benedetto is not actually making the guitars at the Custom Shop, will there be any structural, material or design differences between the Custom Shop Benedetto and the guitars that you make in your shop?

BB: As far as the Custom Shop Benedetto guitar, you won't be able to tell the difference. I'll personally be doing the training, while maintaining close contact in terms of quality control. The guitars will be made and set-up exactly as I do it myself. And, as mentioned before, the guitars that I'll be making at my own shop will all be custom instruments. On those, I expect quite a few design changes.

CC: What kind of vision do you have for your involvement with Guild?

BB: A very clear one—Guild is going to become the leading manufacturer of archtop guitars. I don't say that lightly —it's a commitment.

CC: What about the future of the Benedetto guitar?

BB: The Benedetto name will likewise be brought to another level. This will be a real renaissance for both Guild and me. There's no limit to the possibilities!

Photo by Donna Chapman

Bob Benedetto and Charles at the New York City Jazz Awards debuting the prototype of the Benedetto/Guild Manhattan Model.

George Benson — (June 2000)

Photo by Kwaku Alston

George was born on March 22, 1943 in Pittsburgh, PA. His stepfather, Thomas Collier, taught George to play the ukulele at age six; by age eight he was sitting in with his stepfather singing, dancing and playing the ukulele. In 1954 George was given an electric guitar, and by the time he was 17 was leading his own successful rock and soul band. His interest slowly turned to jazz as he listened intently to records of Django Reinhardt, Charlie Christian, Wes Montgomery and Grant Green. In 1962 Jack McDuff hired him as a sideman and over the next three years he honed his craft playing with many of the foremost jazz performers on the scene at that time.

After Wes Montgomery's death in 1968, Benson was the obvious choice for Creed Taylor (producer of Wes's records) to sign on. Taylor's choice would prove to be right, but success was not actually realized until 1976 when his recording of *Breezin'* passed the 2,000,000 mark. *Breezin'* remains the best-selling jazz album of all time, having now sold over 10 million copies world-wide. He has won just about every jazz poll and award possible and in 1990 Berklee College of Music bestowed their Honorary Doctorate Degree upon him.

George Benson's sound for the millennium definitely has emphasis on his instrumental jazz abili-ties. His new release *Absolute Benson* has only three vocals on its nine tracks and recalls his albums of the early-to-mid 1970s. It is an amalgamation of soul, blues and jazz; and has many critics believing that it just may be George's finest release to date. In spite of his unbelievably hectic schedule I was able to catch up with George at his New Jersey home on June 6, 2000.

Charles Chapman: Since we last spoke in 1998 you have acquired a few new guitars, what are they?

George Benson: I recently acquired a couple of Morotoros and have also added a few solid-body style instruments that are extremely unique and impressive. One is a "Boy London" that is very unique with lace trans-sensor pickups, and the other is from New York luthier Woody Phifer.

CC: You mentioned solid body guitars that you have recently acquired, is this a new interest for you?

GB: Oh no, archtops are my love and passion, I own about 35 wonderful archtops by many different and very talented luthiers. One of my prize possessions is Wes Montgomery's Gibson L5, with the Florentine cutaway, that was pictured on the album cover *Movin Wes*. This was the guitar Wes recorded many of his hits like *Windy* and *Going Out of My Head*; and I used it for a Wes tribute concert at the Hollywood Bowl.

You have to remember that I've been around while all this stuff was being invented. Many times I was one of the first guitarists asked to experiment with sound devices and even guitar synthesizers. On the album *Shape of Things to Come* I used a tone divider. Over the years I've used a few solid body instruments, but I keep coming back to the archtop because that is my thing and my sound, but I'm fascinated with new innovations. As with all musicians, I like to see who's out there and what's new. If I can give them a helping hand I do, but in the end I'm benefiting because it keeps the music fresh and I believe I project that to my audience.

CC: You mentioned before that you like to help up and coming guitarists, have you run into any of late that have caught your attention?

GB: Yes, Serge Krief, he's a French guitarist and is magnificent. Serge is a Django expert and knows everything Django ever played note for note, but he also plays modern jazz like you can't believe. He's never been out there and no one knows of him.

CC: How did you meet Serge?

GB: When I was in France he came to see me at my hotel, we played a little and he just flattened me with his talent. He and his rhythm guitarist, Richard, saved all their money and came to the United States a little while back, I contacted the "Blue Note" and asked if they could play during the breaks. Management graciously agreed and Serge and Richard just tore the house up. Somebody heard them and they were able to get a few good gigs—I wish them the best. Another guy I heard recently that just knocked me out was a young guitar player in Spain. His name was Tomatito, which means little tomato. Man, this guy is just magnificent. His rhythm and tonality and his approach is masterful. He is flamenco, but you still hear jazz, blues and the whole bag.

CC: It must get annoying to have musicians coming up to you all the time wanting something from you?

GB: Yes, I will admit that it is sometimes trying, but most of the time it's a joy. It exposes me to fresh new ideas and I just love the way younger cats awaken something in me from the early days, I love listening and playing with guys like Joshua Redman, Roy Hargrove and Christian McBride. When they tell me I've still got the chops, I feel great.

CC: You must have one of the most diverse audiences I have ever seen, it spans all age groups from teenagers with pink hair to great-grandmothers with blue hair. To what do you credit your popularity among all of these varied ages and musical interests; and the longevity of your career?

GB: We like the same things in life and I let it be known. I'm not afraid to express that. Especially years ago, if you were a jazz guitar player and expressed you liked something else you were put on their crap list. A lot of my old jazz fans were miffed when I achieved pop success. Jazz fans want to be catered to and I've tried that approach and it doesn't work for me. Nobody can stay one way for 30 years. You hear, you change, the door opens and you walk through it. People often forget I was a pop artist when I was a kid and an entertainer before I ever dreamed of being a jazz musician. The easiest way to involve people is by getting them to tap their feet. When they're tapping a bit, they'll go your way. That's when I can float any kind of jazz line into the music. Once the audience knows I respect them, they let me be whatever I want to be.

CC: If memory serves me correctly, a few years ago you were contemplating an alternate career in acting, why did you give it up?

GB: I was actually very into it at one time. I did a number of guest spots on the TV series *Mike Hammer* as well as a few film roles. Quite a few scripts started to come my way and I had to re-evaluate what I really wanted. Even in television you are on the set from 12 to 16 hours a day and I made the decision to put all my efforts in my music and guitar which is really where my heart is.

CC: I understand you have a very interesting story about a Cadillac you own, could you tell us a little about that?

GB: I don't know how interesting it is, but I do own a very unusual and wonderful Cadillac. When I was a kid in Pittsburgh I used to go across town to the Cadillac dealership to check out their cars. In 1959 an experimental car, called the Cyclone, was sent to the dealership to display. I could never get it out of my mind. I used to try to tell people about it and they all thought I was crazy, nobody seemed to have ever heard of it. I thought about that car for over forty years. About eight years ago I realized, 'I'm not poor anymore, why don't I try to find it and buy it.' A dealer found the Cyclone for me and it was unbelievable. It had been in a museum for over thirty years and the wheels had never touched the road. It is a fantastic machine and I immediately bought it.

CC: If you could record with any musician, living or deceased, who would that be?

GB: That's easy, Charlie Parker and Nat King Cole. Playing guitar with Nat King Cole would have been great, but he sure didn't need me because he always had the great Oscar Moore with him.

CC: What is your equipment set up for both live gigs and in the studio?

GB: I use the Ibanez GB20 and the GB12 guitars for live performances. The GB12 is just a beefed up version of the GB10; Ibanez refers to it as the anniversary model. These guitars are consistent and I always know what I'm going to get when I plug them in, I designed them that way! My amplifier setup is a Polytone run in series with a Fender DeVille. The Polytone has been one of my favorite amps since *Breezin'* and the Fender has a very quick response which makes it perfect for the fast things I play. The combination of these two amps, with my Ibanez guitars, gives me just the sound I'm looking for in my live shows.

In the studio I will often use guitars from my collection because I can control the situation and make sure they sound the way they were intended to. I always run direct to get a good clean signal and also place a microphone in front of the amplifier. I want that slight bit of distortion and sustain that comes from the amps to give roundness and that live feeling. I use only Thomastik-Infeld strings. I have worked with the Thomastik people and designed a number of sets that I am very happy with.

CC: What gear did you use on the *Breezin'* session?

GB: I did something on that session that I had never done before or since. I used new equipment that I had never recorded with. It was the first time I recorded with the Polytone as well as my new Johnny Smith guitar. I was taking a chance, but the results are now history.

CC: Did you use any other guitars on that album?

GB: No, the JS was the only guitar used for that project.

CC: How do you feel the recording industry has changed over the years?

GB: When I first came to NY in the 1960s we used to make albums in one or two days at the most. The standard day at Rudi Van Gelders studio was to record from 10 to 1 then take a lunch break and continue from 2 to 5. That was generally the whole album, unless there was some clean-up stuff to do the next day. It was the same for Blue Note, Prestige and Creed Taylor. In the late 80s, early 90s it took us anywhere from six months to a year to record an album of the same length. When we did *Breezin'* in 1976 it cost us 45 thousand dollars for four days recording in LA. That also included the cost of the London and Munich Symphony Orchestras. When I recorded the *Give Me the Night* album with Quincy Jones in the 1980s we spent 450 thousand.

CC: How long have you been on the road, and essentially how much time do you spend touring each year?

GB: I've been on the road for 37 years and tour about 16 to 20 weeks a year.

CC: I just received your new album and think it's one of your best, can you give us your thoughts on it?

GB: Joe Sample was the linchpin in this album and inspired me to play in a different way. He is an extremely musical guy and is one of the reasons why this album is one of my best projects to date. I enjoy playing guitar now more than I ever have and I think it comes out in this album. I'm getting tremendous response from audiences on the road, and a respect from jazz musicians like I have not seen since my early days.

CC: Why do you think that is?

GB: I think musicians have now finally accepted me for what I am, and are no longer trying to force me to be what they think I should be. They see that the public loves me and are actually listening to what I'm trying to do.

Photo by Donna Chapman

Peter Bernstein – (March 1999)

At 32, New York City based Peter Bernstein has established himself as a consummate sideman, as well as a noteworthy leader/recording artist and gifted composer. As a sideman Peter's discography surpasses 30 recordings. He's worked with Joshua Redman, Lou Donaldson, Joe Lavano, Roy Hargrove, Maceo Parker, Jack McDuff and Dr. Lonnie Smith to name a few. To date Peter has recorded four CDs as a leader, for the Criss Cross label, his most recent being *Earth Tones* (Criss 1151 CD).

Peter was originally self taught and later studied with Attila Zoller, Gene Bertoncini and Jim Hall. He majored in jazz studies at Rutgers University with influential coaches Ted Dunbar and Kenny Barron; and holds a degree from The New School in New York City. Peter is simultaneously a member of the Jimmy Cobb's Mob, Lou Donaldson Quartet, Melvin Rhyne Trio, and his own trio featuring Larry Goldings and Bill Stewart.

The following interview was conducted at Peter's home in New York City on March 5, 1999.

Charles Chapman: You've stated in the past that your original influences were Jimi Hendrix and B.B. King. Why and when did you make the switch to jazz?

Peter Bernstein: While I was growing up my parents didn't listen to jazz. They listened to the Beatles, Bob Dylan and that sort of thing. When I first got into guitar Hendrix and all the blues guys were what really turned me on, especially B.B. King. After I had been into guitar for a while I started reading about Joe Pass, Wes Montgomery and definitely Kenny Burrell. So I really got into the jazz guitar sounds and started buying all their albums I could find. Grant Green and Kenny Burrell were huge influences, and I also listened to a lot of organ players like Jimmy Smith and Jack McDuff.

CC: Any particular album that really inspired you?

PB: Definitely Wes Montgomery's *Smokin' At The Half Note, Mellow Mood* and *James and Wes*. Kenny Burrel and John Coltrane, Miles Davis's *Bitches Brew*, then I started going back to Charlie Parker, Fats Navarro, Clifford Brown and got away from guitar players and spent quite a bit of time really getting into horn players.

CC: You have a sense of melody and time very reminiscent of Jim Hall. What exactly has your affiliation with Jim been?

PB: I met Jim when I was going to the New School and studied with him there. Being up close and having the opportunity to play with him was really an experience. In 1990 he asked me to join him in his "Guitar Invitational Concert" at the JVC festival. A recording on the "Music Masters" label came from this. I did a duo with him on a number of occasions including a 1994 European tour, that passed through the "North Sea Jazz Festival" and "Braccon Festival" in Wales. Jim is not your typical guitarist, but what he plays comes from the quality of the guitar, like those open string things he does. If the same lines were played on any other type instrument it would not be the same. He is like a poet and uses the uniqueness of the instrument to really get an original voice on the guitar. That is exactly what I am trying to do now.

CC: You are one of the busiest guitarists on the scene today. Besides being a fine player how do account for this?

PB: It is definitely not my business sense. In fact, I've only recently put my bio and promo package together. I've been very lucky and people have always seemed to call me for gigs. Also I've been fortunate enough to work with guys like Larry (Goldings) and Bill Stewart. We get along well together and try to share and spread the word around when we hear about gigs, concerts, etc. Also, I met a lot of great musicians at the New School that opened a lot of doors for me. I really don't hustle the way I should and I'm just very lucky that the phone keeps ringing.

CC: Do you consider yourself more of a side-man or leader?

PB: Until recently I have definitely been more of a sideman, but I'm working very hard trying to change that. Being a sideman can be limiting because many times you can't control the gigs you get or when the phone rings. I really want to go out on my own more and try to develop my own music and sound, the only way I see to do that is lead my own group.

CC: What guitars do to you use?

PB: Originally I used a Gibson 175, about 1995 I started playing an L5, that's the guitar I used on my recordings with Joshua Redman. Recently I was fortunate enough to acquire a wonderful handmade archtop. It was made by a great Phila-

delphia luthier, John Zeidler. I really love it! It's about twenty years old, completely acoustic with a floating humbucking pickup which they tell me is quite unusual for an acoustic archtop. It looks a lot different than your typical archtop and everywhere I go people are always asking me about it. It's not as cumbersome as the L5 and has a great long scale neck. I use it for everything now, it's definitely part of my sound.

CC: What is your choice in amplifiers?

PB: A Fender Vibrolux. I also have a Pro Reverb, but the Vibrolux is the one I prefer.

CC: Is this the same type setup you use when you record?

PB: Yes it is. I usually just mic the amp. David Baker recorded my album *Light Blue* and did something quite unusual. He put a mic both in front of and behind the amp and got a great sound.

CC: Any future projects you can tell us about?

PB: I recently released an album, *Earth Tones* which I am very excited about. It is my own trio with Bill Stewart and Larry Goldings. Being asked to participate in the "Visiting Artist Program" at Berklee College is also very exciting. There is a chance I will be at the Regatta Bar in Cambridge with Jimmie Cobbs's group the 22nd of June. I also play a lot around New York City in clubs like the Village Vanguard, The Blue Note, Sweet Basil, Iridum and Smalls.

CC: Have you any words of advice for students?

PB: If you can't live without it, then you know it's what's for you. It can't really even be a choice, it just has to be what you need and have to do.

Gene Bertoncini – *(October 1992)*

Gene Bertoncini has been one of the most prolific and popular studio guitarists in New York City for many years. He was the staff guitarist for Johnny Carson *(The Tonight Show)*, Merv Griffin, Jack Parr and just about every show that used a studio band in NYC during this time in history. His duo recordings and performances with bassist Michael Moore have received worldwide recognition. Gene has worked with Benny Goodman, Buddy Rich, Lena Horne, Wayne Shorter, Clark Terry, Ron Carter and too many more to list. He is as comfortable playing jazz on the classical as he is on the steel string electric.

Gene is a widely sought after clinician and has taught at Eastman School of Music, The New England Conservatory and the Baniff School of Fine Arts in Alberta, Canada. The following interview took place at Gene's home in New York City on September 12, 1992.

Charles Chapman: Who or what influenced you the most in your career as a guitarist?

Gene Bertoncini: My earliest influence was my first teacher, Johnny Smith. He taught me respect for the fingerboard and music in general.

CC: I didn't realize Johnny Smith lived in New York City for any amount of time?

GB: Oh yes, he was on the staff at NBC. At that time radio shows were very popular and involved a lot of reading, so only the best players worked there. As a kid I was doing local television and used to hang around the studios. One day I popped into his studio and played for him and after that he used to give me lessons for free. This was during the time when he made that great *Moonlight in Vermont* record. It was a great gift to hang onto the coat-tails of a man as talented as him. After Johnny I studied with Chuck Wayne, he also had a major influence on my career.

CC: If I remember correctly, he had a very different right hand picking technique.

GB: Yes, his picking technique was completely opposite of what Johnny used. His idea was to sort of slur over the strings instead of using alternate picking, letting the pick float in the direction of the scale you were playing.

CC: Did you convert to that technique?

GB: I used Johnny's for a while, then I practiced Chuck's for a while, then I combined them both and now I'm totally confused (laughs). Seriously, I really feel that a combination of both is the best way to go.

CC: I've always enjoyed the way you play the nylon string guitar. How did you get started in that direction?

GB: That was Chuck's influence. One day he told me to listen to Julian Bream. I went out and bought an album called: *The Art of Julian Bream*, and one cut, *Pavanne for a Dead Princess*, haunted me. I listened to it over and over again until I finally decided that I just had to study that style of guitar. I was very lucky because the classical guitar at that time in history was fairly new to most listeners.

CC: What made you choose *Embraceable You* as your contribution to the Harvie Swartz project *In a Different Light*?

GB: Actually Harvie chose that one.

CC: I enjoyed the way Harvie played the melody with a bow and you comped behind him. Was that your idea?

GB: No, it was Harvie's. I've had a long standing duo with Michael Moore who uses the bow marvelously. Harvie may have arrived at the idea by listening to the duo.

CC: How is the studio scene in New York City?

GB: It is slower than in past years, but it seems to be picking up. Producers are starting to use players rather than synthesizers.

CC: What do you find the most satisfying aspect of your career?

GB: I'm really glad that I started playing jazz on the nylon string guitar because I find it extremely satisfying and lends itself beautifully for solo guitar playing. The most fulfilling part is being able to play a single line and comp for myself. When it works the way I hear it—it is just wonderful!

When I was much younger I would listen to the Oscar Peterson Trio, and contemplate how easy it would be for a guitar to replace the piano and wonder why it wasn't done more often. The most challenging part of guitar is being able to stand on your own and be aware of what you are doing in terms of melody and harmony. Here lately I've been trying to play melody on the bottom strings and comp over that. Tuck Andress is the one who has really inspired me to go in that direction.

CC: What was your most recent musical challenge?

GB: I played a couple of nights solo guitar in a jazz club in Toronto called the Guitar Bar which features only guitar players. That was a great challenge. I also played a solo concert in Denver where they have a guitar workshop and I was the only jazz guitarist.

CC: Any words of advice to aspiring guitarists who will be reading this?

GB: The most important aspect to playing music is to really be in touch with the notes you hear. As guitarists we have a tendency to learn a lot about the instrument and have it play us. Guitar is very complex and we sometimes just end up playing in position and not the notes we really hear. As soon as possible develop your ear on the guitar and let that take you where you want to go.

Photo by Donna Chapman

Photo by Donna Chapman

Gene Bertoncini and Charles back stage at a New York City concert.

Photo by Donna Chapman

Kenny Poole and Gene Bertoncini in concert.

23

Kevin Eubanks – *(November 1995)*

Kevin Eubanks must have one of the highest profiles of any guitarist in America. He's viewed by millions, five nights a week as the guitarist, musical director and sidekick to Jay Leno on NBC's *The Tonight Show.*

Kevin comes from a very musical family in Philadelphia, PA. His mother has an advanced degree in music and his two uncles Tommy and Ray Bryant being prominent jazz musicians in their own right. Kevin's first instrument was violin which he studied for six years before switching to guitar. He was playing local gigs when he was thirteen, and after graduating from high school in 1975 was accepted to Berklee College of Music. Berklee is where he originally met Branford Marsalis and they forged a musical and personal relationship that has lasted many years.

At 37 Kevin is already a seasoned veteran, with 12 albums and stints with jazz luminaries like Art Blakey, Roy Haynes and McCoy Tyner. It wasn't until Branford Marsalis asked him to join forces to form the new Tonight Show Band that he came to the national limelight. In January of 1995 Branford left *The Tonight Show* to pursue his concert and recording career, which he felt was being jeopardized by the rigors of a national TV show. Leno,

among others decided to give Kevin a try at being in the catbird seat, and he has surpassed everyone's expectations. The following interview was conducted on the set of *The Tonight Show* in Burbank, CA on— November 1, 1995.

Charles Chapman: I'm sure I'm not the only guitar player who has watched and listened to you on *The Tonight Show* and muttered—what are those great-sounding guitars Kevin is playing? Could you shed some light on those very unique instruments?

Kevin Eubanks: My guitars are all made by Abe Rivera a friend of mine from Long Island, New York. Pat Martino uses his guitars and, in fact, that's how I met Abe. He's made many guitars for me; I own a few archtops, a couple of flat-tops, a classical, and of course the solidbody. On the acoustics he uses curly maple for the back and sides, spruce for the top, and maple for the neck. I'm not sure what the solidbody is made of because that was a gift from Abe.

CC: What types of pickups or micing system do you use?

KE: My archtops are fitted with SHAZ-49 Zoller archtop pickups made by Shadow, and I only mic my flat-tops. I haven't found an acoustic pickup or micing system that I like so I just use an AKG 451 external mic for the flat-tops. On my solidbody, I have two Seymour Duncan pick-ups. I use D'Addario strings on all my guitars; flat-wounds on the archtops, starting at .013, roundwounds on my flat-tops starting at .012 and .011's on my electric.

CC: What amplifiers and effects do you use on *The Tonight Show?*

KE: My amps are the Duel Rectifier and Blue Angel from MESA/Boogie. The effects I commonly use are the Mesa V-Twin, Pro-Co Rat, Cry Baby, BOSS Octave Dividers, Chorus Ensemble, Tremolo Pan and one of their volume pedals. I mainly use the Rat for distortions, but the Dual Rectifier and the Mesa V-Twin are also used for distortion. I have to have different types to fit the tune that I'm playing.

CC: The rigors of a gig like yours must be much more than what we see on television. What are your responsibilities as bandleader, and about how much time do you spend a day on the studio set?

KE: It's relentless. I have to keep the music fresh, play behind visiting artists, and write music for many of the comedy skits. I'm generally there six to eight hours a day.

CC: You have great players in the band, do you resent that you're not given the chance to actually perform and stretch out, or was it just a given when you took the gig that the situation would be as it is?

KE: There's no resentment at all. I knew what the job was when I excepted it—you don't go to a Chinese restaurant and order Italian. I'm very happy having the caliber of players I have, we're all professionals and we all know what is expected of the job. People always ask that question and I really don't understand it. We all do outside gigs and recordings, and that is where we get our chance to stretch out.

CC: Do you plan on staying with *The Tonight Show* gig indefinitely or do you have a time frame with the show?

KE: Right now I plan on staying indefinitely. It's a good gig, after being on the road for 15 years you appreciate being able to stay in one place and go to your own home at night. Can't beat that!

Kevin as a student at Berklee.

Kevin with luthier Kirk Sands.

25

Jon Finn – *(March 1998)*

Photo by Teresa Izzo

Jon Finn is surely one of the busiest guitarists in the New England area; working constantly and receiving kudos from critics and musicians alike for his virtuosic technique and soulful melodies.

His first album with The Jon Finn Group *Don't Look So Serious* was released in 1994 to deservedly rave reviews; and in May 1997, he finished a six month stint as guitarist for the Boston production of the Broadway smash *Rent*. He also preforms and records with the world famous Boston Pops Orchestra under the direction of Keith Lockheart. If all that weren't enough, Jon is one of the most sought-after guitar instructors at Berklee College in Boston.

Like I said Jon's a busy guy. So with a new release *Wicked*, on the way and Jon's popularity growing we thought this would be a good time to have a chat.

Charles Chapman: Every time I see you in concert you're playing a different guitar and have altered your rig. Is there something you're searching for in the way of sound?

Jon Finn: Changing guitars and altering my rig comes from the ultimate quest for tone and an innate curiosity. I only play Ibanez guitars and

have endorsed them since 1993. At the moment I am playing two electric guitars, both the new S Classic Series. The first is right off the production line and the second is a custom-built model, specifically made for me. The custom guitar has three pickups where the standard S has only two. Also, the custom has a whammy bar and Seymour Duncan pickups. I'm also endorsed by Laney. When I initially received the endorsement I used a VC50 which is a 2 X 12, 50-watt combo. More recently I've been using the VC30 which is a smaller 2 X 10 model. My stage setup is a wet/dry configuration. My guitar signal goes into the combo amp, and then I send line from the combo amp through a Lexicon LXP15. This goes to a power amp which powers two 4 X 12 cabinets. The reason I do this is that the combo gives you the direct open-back, no-effects, no-bull sound. The cabs with the effects give the ambience that is required for the particular tune. It's nice because you get all the effects without compromising the guitar sound in the process.

CC: You rarely see guitarists who perform in the progressive rock circle being asked to do theater and orchestra work. Do you need to have a different mind set in these types of gigs and how does your equipment setup differ?

JF: You definitely have to have a different mindset. First of all, you are providing a supporting role. The thing about *Rent* and the Boston Pops is that they are both large-scale productions. You have to realize that you are a cog in the wheel and totally have to be a team player—even more than on the usual gig. You must really have your own technical act together as well. In these large productions you must know what sound you want and know how to get it. When you bring your rig to the sound people, you must be able to tell them exactly what is needed. In the *Rent* show, I used the Laney VC30 amp which was miced, and my acoustic guitar went directly into the PA.

CC: You did a series of acoustic duo concerts with Larry Mitchell. Do you have any future plans with Larry and do you plan to incorporate acoustic guitar into future projects?

JF: It was great performing with Larry and I will work with him anytime he calls. The new record has one tune on it where I'm using a nylon-string acoustic and I do plan to incorporate more acoustic guitar in future projects.

CC: What acoustic guitars do you use and how do you amplify them?

JF: I use both steel and nylon string Ibanez acoustic guitars. I have a strong preference for running acoustics direct into the sound system and never using an amp. With the Ibanez onboard electronics, I get the best sound using this method.

CC: What are your plans for the upcoming year?

The Jon Finn Band live in concert.

JF: First and foremost is to finish the album and schedule a short tour to promote it. It also looks good that I will be spending time performing in England, Germany and possibly a few other countries. The Boston Pops have asked me to do a few gigs in the 1998 season and one of my main goals is to get the band (The Jon Finn Band) out playing as much as possible. I will also continue to write my monthly column for *Guitar* magazine and teach full-time at Berklee. Looks like it's going to be another busy year.

Photo by Donna Chapman

Jon and Charles at the Ibanez booth at a trade show.

27

Mitch Holder – (2000)

Photo by Bob Barry

The name Mitch Holder may not be commonplace, especially if you're one of those east coast guys like myself, but I can guarantee you're familiar with his work and probably have seen him many times without even realizing it. Mitch has been one of the most sought after studio guitarists in the LA area for over twenty-five years and is still going strong. The problem with trying to write an article of someone of Mitch Holder's stature is: Where the hell do I start! I had a similar problem with an interview I recently did with Carol Kaye, another great musician and also a partner of Mitch's in the wonderful CD project *Thumbs Up*. Well, my apologies for all those I leave out, but here's a brief synopsis of artists and projects Mitch has garnered so far in his career.

He has performed on recordings with Barbara Streisand, Dionne Warwick, Lee Ritenour, Lionel Ritchie, Stevie Nicks, Michael McDonald, Herbie Hancock and Anita Baker. To date he has performed on five platinum and over twenty-five gold records. His film scores and soundtracks include: *Space Cowboys, On Golden Pond, Back to the Future, Mrs. Doubtfire* and *Indiana Jones and the Temple of Doom*. On TV his very distinctive guitar work permeates many great shows: *Cheers, Murder She Wrote, Picket Fences, Coach, Barney Miller, Tiny Toon Adven-*

tures, *The Simpsons*, and the list goes on and on. Mitch also writes, arranges and has taught in many different venues including USC , as well as being a Gibson consultant, product specialist, and clinician. His most visible gig was with the Tonight Show band with Johnny Carson where he performed full or part time from 1974 through 1988.

Through his formative years he mentored under William Pellegrini, Johnny Frisco, George Van Eps and Howard Roberts. He gives homage to Barney Kessel, Wes Montgomery as well as citing Link Wray and Duane Eddy for early influences in developing a simple, direct approach to melody and tone. When you speak with Mitch he is a very humble guy (as most of the great players are) and he is still a very young man who has not even started to slow down.

Early in the new millennium Mitch and I shared numerous e-mails and spoke on several occasions; the following are Mitch's thoughts on performing, gear and the musicians life in general, from the consummate professional.

Charles Chapman: I'm told you own upward of 100 guitars. Are you a collector or just a musician with a huge passion for guitars?

Mitch Holder: Well, the true number is more like 60, but I don't consider myself a real guitar collector. I have a particular instrument for a specific reason, either for a particular sound, as part of my studio work or for jazz playing, which is where my roots are. I have also had a keen interest in guitar design going back to my very early years and have had several prototypes built.

CC: Tell us about the Gibson guitar known in the industry as the ES-357.

MH: The ES-357 came out of the period in the late '70s when the guitar of the decade in the studios was the Gibson 335 and new synthesizers coming out were covering the same frequency as the guitar. These new synth sounds wound up canceling out the guitars on the playbacks and we all had to scramble to find something that would cut through. That guitar turned out to be the Strat, and with its middle pickup, you could get in a range that blended well with the synths. I thought Gibson should market a three pickup 335 for people who wanted a Straty sound, but wanted to still play a Gibson type guitar. I worked with Tim Shaw and Bruce Bolen, in R&D at Gibson (now both with the Guild Custom Shop) and came up with the ES-357. It's based on the ES-5 and the ES-347 with no F-holes (to cut down on feedback) and three P-90 pickups. It has the three volumes and one tone, set up like a late 347, with a mini toggle (to control the middle pickup) by the regular toggle. The sound of the guitar is truly unique. Nothing I've played sounds like it and it's brighter than the ES-5 because of the internal block and stop tailpiece. It has a fine tune TP-6 tailpiece that I really like because you can tune the guitar with your right hand without taking your left hand off the strings. This was great in the middle of a take when I felt a little tuning tweaking was needed, but didn't want to kill a sustaining note. I used that guitar a lot in the studios when I got it in '83, several studio guys heard it and wanted one. When I decided to have a spare built, five studio guys requested one as well, and a small run was made. An article and picture appeared in *Guitar Player Magazine* and a few more were ordered from that. I have no idea how many 357s were actually built, as Kalamazoo closed down in '84 and the rest came out of Nashville. It was very chaotic at Gibson back then and the record keeping got a bit neglected.

CC: Do you still own or have you ever owned any vintage archtops that you consider memorable?

MH: I did have a '34 L-5 that I put a DeArmond pickup on to make an electric out of that frustrated me to no end, but the guitar acoustically was a monster. This was in the 60s and I was about 15 when I bought it and didn't know any better and sold it when I couldn't get it to sound right amplified. My heartthrob is the Epiphone Howard Roberts Custom that I still play and used on the *Thumbs Up Trio* CD with Carol Kaye and Ray Pizzi. I started taking lessons from Howard in '66. He had played his own HR Custom at Donte's (a well known jazz supper club here in L.A.) where I first saw it and then he pulled it out at a lesson one day. I had been using a Gibson ES-175D at the time and the HR guitar felt similar as it was the same size, but had a longer scale fingerboard (25½" vs 24¾" on the 175) which appealed to my large hands. I waited about a year for that guitar and when I got it and let Howard play it, he looked at me real funny. Finally

I said "Howard, what's the matter?" He proceeded to tell me about the first HR Custom that Epi (president of Epiphone guitars) had sent him that he really liked (It's the one on the cover of his Capitol recording, *Goodies*), and it had been stolen from a session. Howard felt mine played just like that one. In another few years he switched alliance to Gibson and, ironically, I acquired the oval holed prototype of that series from his wife last year. I used it acoustically in the opening of the movie *Space Cowboys*, recording a tune that Clint Eastwood had written for the film. It's just a fabulous guitar and it definitely has Howard's karma. I've had a couple of spiritual visits from him, showing me some things. It didn't surprise me as I've felt Howard's presence since he passed on. He was one of a kind and I miss him and his playing and antics immensely. There are hundreds of guitarists that were influenced by him.

CC: What guitar or guitars do you consider your mainstay working guitars?

MH: In the studios it's still the Strats and whatever electrics or acoustics, banjos, mandolins, etc. are needed. They're tools to me, whatever it takes to get the job done. I have two large cases just for all the instruments. For jazz it's either one of the HR's, or a thin bodied '96 Wes Montgomery L-5 I'm very fond of. It's Byrdland size with one pickup and a full scale board and is a real gem; sounds great and is oh, so comfortable. I've been using John Pearse strings for quite a few years now and they've been just great. The acoustic strings are the best sounding I've heard and after using them, I gravitated to the electrics as well and they really sound wonderful—and last too. I like Thomastiks for classical guitar; they have a model, the Classic C Series, that doesn't stretch out when you first put them on and I can attest that they work.

CC: What is your live rig like and how does that differ in the studio?

MH: That's like night and day. For live I'll use a jazz guitar or the ES-357 or ES-355 straight into the amp. Fender London Reverb or old Paul Riveraized Princeton that weighs hardly anything and can blow the roof off, if need be. I just love the relationship of a guitar and an amp, your body and hands make up the rest of the sound. I've always thought that effects mask the real individuality of a player and that's why it's hard to pick out who's playing on some of the stuff that we have done over the years. It all started sounding the same because everyone was using the same effects. I was very happy when synths came along and took over all the 'sound effects.' Before that it was "Hey guitar player, what crazy, goofy sound do you have?" and off we'd go trying to come up with something crazy enough to appease them. Went with the territory and that's where good attitude comes to play, I always tried to have a smile on my face, going through all the multitudes of trying this sound and that wah and this filter and that squak and doink.

Contrary to the live rig, my studio rig, in addition to the two instrument cases, is an effects rack (TC M-2000, Eventide H3000, Yamaha SPX 90, DBX Compressor, Hush II). I use an Egnator ie4 preamp (4 separate preamps in a three rack space) and a stomp box shelf that pulls out (Ibanez Tube Screamer, Ibanez Analog Delay, TC Phasor, Small Stone Phasor, TC Chorus, Boss Octaver, Boss Touch Wah, MXR DynaComp,). Also, a Vox Cry Baby and two Goodrich volume pedals, one right after the guitar and one on the output. I use a Ground Control Footswitcher going to a Ground Control Systems mixer in the rack. This all goes to a VHT 2150 power amp and then through two EV 12" cabinets. The rack was built by rack guru, David Friedman at Rack Systems in North Hollywood. There's also an old Music Man 210/65 amp on standby as well. I've also been into the Line 6 Pod, and it works great as a direct recording tool without the need for an amp. I had a chance to try it at Capitol and the engineer loved the sound, thought it was a miced amp. Amp modeling has really become a wonderful thing and a very useful tool. Some people say they don't quite sound like the real deal, but I don't know anybody who owns all those amps and I think you'd have to go a long way to hear any difference in a track.

CC: How does session work differ today than in the past?

MH: The whole studio scene has changed out here. Some of that is due to the obvious changes in recording technology and some of it is the result of the politics of the business that went down in the '80s. All these people with garages filled with new MIDI gear were coaxing the production work away from each other, by bringing their prices down to a point where the producers got real comfortable. That's the status quo now and there's not much money in today's budgets to hire outside players,

so the work has gotten pretty spotty. In the late '70s there were several years where I was doing an average of 600 three-hour sessions per year. There were several industry strikes, including the musicians in 1980, that was the first dent in the armor. Then MIDI came out and sampling followed and now there's Pro Tools (a hard drive recording, editing software package) which everyone uses and, poof, not much work for players. What I miss the most from the early days was the incredible creative process of playing together. The producers would call a rhythm section for several days of laying down tracks. An arranger would listen to the parts that were generated, and write the overdubbed horns and/or string parts and anything else from that. Everything is controlled and stacked now and there aren't many opportunities for going for something, or a lucky accident, or any of that. I miss the way we all bounced off of each other coming up with parts; it just doesn't happen much anymore, everything is done under a microscope. The best feeling in the world was walking out of the studio knowing how good it felt to play with that particular group of musicians and come up with something really special, that wasn't necessarily intended, it just jelled and came together. That I miss more than anything.

CC: Is there any particular session or gig that stands out in your mind, either good or bad?

MH: For me, the best sessions I had were on several movie soundtracks with composer/pianist Dave Grusin. He is at the top of my list of musicians who, in their career, could do it all. Play incredibly, both jazz and legit, and be able to write/arrange and conduct. His melodies from those dates still pop in my head, which to me makes it very special, as I don't tend to remember a lot once it's done and I'm gone. I'll never forget his words of instruction to me during the *On Golden Pond* sessions. On one cue he said "Mitch, why don't you SAY this," and played what he wanted on the piano. Just the way he said those words had quite an impact on me. I never heard that expression from anyone else except him; and what it said to us was how much he respected us, which was an incredible feeling from someone like that, who we all gave the utmost respect. He's the only composer I ever saw get an ovation from the entire orchestra!

CC: At the present do you still make the majority of your living in the studio?

MH: I still do studio work, but the drastic reduction has forced me to be involved with playing and doing some of my own recording plus some other interesting projects. I also do some writing and have been involved with a new guitar company for the last few years, that my partners and myself are trying to get off the ground.

CC: At a young age you have had an incredible career. Where do you hope to go from here and what are some of the musical goals you would like to achieve?

MH: I'm in a transitional phase at this point; after so many years in the studios, getting back to my roots in jazz and pursuing the guitar company, doing a little studio work and some other recording projects. However, I'm also quite concerned about the status of jazz education and awareness in the lower grade levels. I feel that the college level is well represented as far as producing qualified musicians. Now what we need is a new generation of young, educated folks to make sure that jazz survives. The focus has been on generating musicians, now we need to generate an audience. Classical music is also crying for some new music. There's just no financial motivation for composers. All those qualified writers are making their living composing for movies or TV or whatever. There aren't too many fresh interpretations of the existing repertoire that hasn't already been done. I've been talking to some educators and music foundations in an attempt to get it going, and hope that it could become successful enough to go into schools nationwide.

CC: What advice would you give a young guitarist wanting to make a career in music and specifically as a studio guitarist?

MH: The days of being a freelance guitar player, just doing studio work are over. Today's musicians have to be qualified in many areas; computer skills, writing, recording, arranging, etc. Having a good business sense is very important, for purposes of survival; and a good attitude is a given. I've also recently become aware of some younger people who are very adept at using the technology to come up with altogether new ways of using all that's available. They've grown up with electronic instrument technology and hear a new world of musical sounds, they have the knowledge to create what they're hearing. I also believe we have a whole new generation of listeners that have a very 'perfect'

sense of time from growing up listening to drum machines on records. When real drummers appeared again I think the human time variance came back to play, and those listeners got adjusted to both camps. I feel that's fine, the human and electronic worlds can co-exist and us humans can accommodate whatever fresh aspects come of it. That's progress and you can rant and rave about it all you want, but you can't stop it, history proves that. It's up to us to adjust to it and utilize it in a way that satisfies our creative urges, whatever they may be.

CC: Could you briefly comment on your approach to improvising?

MH: That's a topic I'm very interested in. Many players of all instruments tend to focus a lot on what scales work with what chords. The first order of business is to work with the chordal tones, as the best melodic devices will come out of those notes. One of the most beneficial exercises that worked for me and my students was to put the guitar down, listen to the changes, say 4 or 8 measures at a time, and think of a melody line in your head. Something that really appeals to you without worrying about what scale it came from. Then once it's set pick up the guitar and play it, no matter how long it takes, just work at it until you get that line you thought up in your head. After awhile of doing this you will gradually put it all together at a faster pace, and all of a sudden start playing what you hear rather than what you figure out. That's where your own style comes from. You do, of course, have to learn the scales, arpeggios, modes, etc., but then let that go and play what you hear and feel. The idea is to be able to freely translate what's in your mind to the fingerboard of the guitar without getting yourself all fouled up; although that happens sometimes anyway. My motto is; if you don't hit some 'wrong' notes once in awhile, you're not trying hard enough. That's live, of course, in the studio you have to strive for perfection, although they can 'fix' anything now through digital editing.

CC: What are your thoughts on guitarists learning to read and how important is it in the studio?

MH: It's crucial and expected now. When I first started just being able to read got you work, but now it's a given. When bass synths became predominant in the '80s, we were doubling a lot of those parts. They would give you the bass part, so you would have to be able to read bass clef as well.

The more you can do, the more styles you can play, the more valuable you become. Besides that, music notation has been around for hundreds of years. It is an important method of communicating and learning music that can be passed down from generation to generation. I have nothing against tablature, I just find it interesting that guitar is the only instrument that uses it. You don't find violin players learning by tab. Trust me, it isn't that difficult to learn to read standard notation; it's just that most guitar players learn enough to play some things and then think reading is too hard, boring, or just get lazy and never learn. Once you learn it though, you have all the written music from many centuries available to you as well as the ability to write it down yourself. Tab is the easy way out... just my 2 cents.

CC: Could you tell us a little about upcoming projects, gigs, etc.

MH: At present I'm involved with a new comedy show on Showtime. A buddy of mine that I've worked with for years, Larry Cansler, is music director and I'm the leader/contractor of the band. We'll be doing the pilot right around the time you read this. I'm also playing with an exciting new big band with Chris Walden, a young composer/arranger from Germany. I met him back in '93 when he came out here from Cologne, with his producer, to do an album. They used an L.A. rhythm section and then went back to Germany to do the overdubs. A few years later Chris called and said he'd moved out here. I've done some projects with him, at his elaborate home studio, on some TV movies. Then he started his new big band. It is very challenging music, which Chris either wrote or arranged. We had our first, very successful, gig at Catalina's Bar & Grill in January of '99. Chris wants to record the band sometime in the near future. It reminds me more of an east coast sound than the typical west coast laid back thing (although L.A. is anything but laid back these days). Something else I'm shopping around is a project with two other musicians; Stu Goldberg a fine jazz pianist, composer/arranger, producer and Ira Nepus a fine trombonist that is involved here in L.A. with the Clayton/Hamilton big band. Our project, called Udu, features the three of us doing contemporary American/World music. We've been investigating some avenues of sounds and production to come up with what we hope is a viable, musical identity that hasn't been done before. It's really a culmination of our back-

grounds in jazz, composition and the modern world of recording. We've got material picked out, written by the three of us, and where it goes is wide open at the moment. For the initial tunes, I play electric and acoustic guitars plus some mandolin. We're shopping around for a label and hope to get it out soon. Of course I want to continue playing jazz, and hopefully get a chance to do a solo record at some point. There's still a lot of things ahead to look forward to.

Mitch during an LA studio session sometime during the 1970s.

Thumbs Up Trio

32

Carol Kaye – (1999)

In the annals of studio musicians one name is synonymous with talent, professionalism and longevity—the great bassist Carol Kaye.

For over four decades Ms. Kaye has remained active in an industry that daily spits out the strongest, brightest and the most talented like watermelon seeds at a small town picnic. She broke the barriers of the "old boy studio club" when women were rarely permitted admission, and were virtually never were seen performing on the electric bass. When Carol started to appear in the L.A. studios many old timers must have thought she was beamed down by aliens preparing to invade their domain.

Carol Kaye is truly a Renaissance woman. She started her own publishing company (Gwen Publishing now owned by Alfred), recorded instructional audio and video material before it was fashionable, and solely supported her family before the term single parent was ever coined.

Carol is one of the most recorded musicians in history, with over 10,000 documented sessions, and probably many more that were not in the record books. It is easier to list who she hasn't played with than who she has. Her resume is twenty-two pages

long and I have the sinking feeling that is the abridged version. Let's just say she has performed with everyone from Joe Cocker and The Beach Boys to Frank Sinatra, Joe Pass and Barbara Streisand. Her film and TV credits are so extensive I have no idea where to begin.

I always had the dream of one day being hired to do an L.A. studio session and there, sitting in the bass chair would be Carol Kaye. That I'm sorry to say, has never come to fruition, but last year I turned a corner at the NAMM show and there she was. I had a brief, but very pleasant conversation with her and have since corresponded numerous times and have found her to be a kind and a very sharing person. To my utter embarrassment I learned that she started out as a jazz guitarist; continued playing guitar throughout her career, both live and on records, and still performs on guitar quite frequently. Being a jazz guitarist, music journalist and a devotee of jazz guitar history, I found this quite a humbling experience.

The following is a very brief chronicle of Ms. Kaye's tremendous career as a guitarist, through conversations and documentation she has generously provided.

When Carol was fourteen she decided to seriously study the guitar and went to Horace Hatchett for lessons. Horace was one of the finest teachers in the area, whose students were some of the most notable guitarists of the day such as Howard Roberts and Oscar Moore. Growing up in the housing projects of Wilmington, CA money was in short supply, so Carol worked out a deal to teach at Horace's studio for lessons. One of the first things she learned was to voice chords with only three notes over the standard tune *Blue Skies*. Many now refer to this style of chord accompaniment as Freddie Green rhythm. Horace immediately taught her to notate and read music and not just play by rote. Carol started transcribing Charlie Christian solos from Benny Goodman records immersing herself in that genre. Jazz guitar fascinated her and she was determined not only to learn how to play it, but understand the inner workings as well. Horace also used many of the George Smith chord melody arrangements in his teaching, which filled in the harmonic side of her guitar development. George

Smith was a prominent studio guitarist who specialized in chord melody arrangements. In her teaching Carol used a lot of George Smith's material as well as transcribed solos of Charlie Christian and Django Reinhardt. She would often transcribe instrumental solos from the great Artie Shaw band for study as well. Carol was, and still is, a great fan of Artie Shaw's music.

In her late teens Carol became the guitarist for a very popular seventeen-piece band that did quite a bit of traveling. She learned from many of the seasoned pros in the band, and started to get guitar features building her reputation as a strong instrumentalist. She got bit by the "bebop bug" and started to play with small local jazz groups in and around her Southern California home. She played with many of the best jazz musicians developing her chops as well as her recognition. Over the years Carol played guitar in jazz clubs with Jack Sheldon, Teddy Edwards, Billy Higgins, The Jimmy Smith Trio, and later with Page Cavenaugh just to name a few. Playing jazz was fun and fulfilling, but didn't pay the bills so she had to work a day job to support her mother and children.

In 1957 Carol was working with Beverly Caverns/ Teddy Edwards jazz group featuring Billy Higgins and Curtis Counce, when one night record producer Bumps Blackwell stopped by. He was impressed with the way Carol played, and was interested in hiring her on a regular basis to work in the studios. She really wasn't interested, because it was a known fact that once you went into the studio it could burn you out and, even though you could make good money your "jazz chops" would definitely suffer. She was very apprehensive and not really looking forward to her new found endeavor, but tired of working a day job Carol saw this as an opportunity to make a full time living in music.

Carol's first studio session was with Sam Cooke. It went so well that she went out and bought a solid body guitar, a new amp and other equipment she knew would be necessary in the studio. Shortly after that she played on the Ritchie Valens mega hit *La Bamba*. She found the caliber of musicians much better than she had anticipated, and even though the music wasn't jazz, it could really groove.

She had many hits with Phil Spector (*Zippity DO DA* and other hits with groups such as the Ronettes,

Shirelles, Crystals, Righteous Bros. etc.), Jan & Dean, Sonny & Cher, early OJ's, Duayne Eddy, Pat Boone, Dick Dale, surf-rock groups, early Mongo Santamaria/Willie Bobo, Cannonball Adderly, Howard Roberts, Ike & Tina Turner, Ann-Margaret, Rosemary Clooney, Paul Anka, etc. (see the guitar hits list on the website: http://www.carolkaye.com).

In late 1963 Carol worked a few Motown record dates during which her accidental switch to bass occurred. The bass player did not show up for a session, and someone loaned Carol a bass to play the part. Since she was a guitarist and not a bass player she used a pick—which was unheard of at that time. She had a great time, and everyone loved the sound and groove, and the rest is history.

Since then the majority of Carol's work has been on bass, but she has never put down the guitar and still loves those jazz guitar sounds she heard when she was a child.

Carol graciously agreed to a little Q & A session to give a little more insight into what makes this very talented musician tick.

Charles Chapman: What advice would you give to female musicians on how to cope in what is still predominantly a male industry.

Carol Kaye: Let the men be men....don't have a chip on your shoulder, but DO have a good sense of humor and some witty replies, have your playing together so they can't legitimately complain about it. Just keep the blinders on and don't "fraternize." Always keep it professional, friendly...but with a little wall up. Don't take any off-beat comments to heart (yes, it's hard sometimes) but feed it back to them if it gets a little rough. For instance, a light comment was made to me only once "you sure play great for a girl"...well I liked that person a lot so let him off easy with "and you play great for a guy." The guys all roared.

CC: Who are a few jazz guitarists on the scene today that has caught your attention?

CK: Joe Beck, Bruce Foreman, Mark Whitfield and some others in that same soul-way of playing jazz vein. I love Mundell Lowe's playing and, Mitch Holder whom I work with is also great. I tend to stay away from the "athletes" on guitar (just mainly chops) and go for the creativity. You can say a lot with well-placed notes with a lot of space. And there's a few I hear on the radio, but actually pay more attention to the sax players. I thought Emily Remler had a lot of promise, she was certainly wonderful in her chordal soloing.

CC: What is your all time favorite session?

CK: Well that's hard to pinpoint, there's so many different styles of music to pick and I had some nice hits on guitar too. I'm fond of my rhythm guitar on Wayne Newton's *Danke Shoen,* but think I like my bass things a little better. Some of my favs are: *Feelin' Alright* Joe Cocker, *The Way We Were* Barbara Streisand, *Games People Play* and *Come On Home* Mel Torme, *I Don't Need No Doctor, Heat of the Night* and several other hits with Ray Charles, *Little Green Apples* OC Smith, *Wichita Lineman* Glen Campbell, *Godfather Theme* Andy Williams, *Peace of Mind* Nancy Wilson, and a few of the Beach Boys things (believe it or not) I like Brian Wilson, he was a wonderful composer. And *Hikky Burr,* the wild bass part I cut on Bill Cosby's hit (was almost all improvised, Quincy Jones arrangement, was also the theme of Bill Cosby's 1st TV show 1970). Several movie & TV film things I'm quite proud of: *Thomas Crown Affair, Pawnbroker, Airport, Walk Don't Run, Change of Habit, Across 110th St., Mission Impossible, Kojak, McCloud, Ironside, Streets of San Francisco, MASH,* etc. Sorry, I can never pick out "a favorite." There's so much great music to choose from...all cut with the greatest musicians, composers, arrangers, producers, it's a group effort. The variety is endless.

CC: Was there anyone that you particularly enjoyed working with either in the studios or live?

CK: I played live with Hampton Hawes, fantastic jazz pianist (bass, early 70s), that was a biggie. And enjoyed working for some of the greatest people: Michel LeGrand, Dave Grusin, John Williams, John Prince, Billy Goldenberg, Bob Alcivar, Jerry Goldsmith, Quincy Jones, Jack Hayes and Leo Shuken (who carefully guided Quincy in the rote process of films back then..they admired him so much), Perry Botkin, Walter Scharf, the list goes on and on; such great men, such fine talents.....who make it a challenge and thrill to adequately play their fine music.

CC: Do you have a favorite jazz guitarist (does not have to be living)?

CK: I'd say Joe Pass...but Howard Roberts was great too. And also the fine Wes Montgomery and Barney Kessel, it's hard to have only "one favorite."

CC: Through your career was there any one jazz guitar that you found particularly memorable, and what equipment are you currently using?

CK: My favorite jazz guitar was a non-cutaway Epiphone Emperor with a suspended DeArmond pickup. A beautiful great sounding instrument. I am currently playing an Aria Pro II 4-string electric bass (Steve Baily model), with Thomastik jazz flat wound strings. The amp I use is a Polytone Mini Brute IV.

CC: Can you tell us about any projects, gigs, etc. that you are currently involved in?

CK: I am currently playing some nice live bass concert gigs with Ray Pizzi and Mitch Holder - our album *Thumbs Up* is out and doing nicely. Plus some record dates, private teaching and teaching at the fine Henry Mancini Institute at UCLA. I am completing my *Jazz Improv for Bass* (27th tutorial), and have been busy with film interviews (personal documentary is on-going), as well as with Message Board on my website: www.carolkaye.com, which is fun. My *Jazz Guitar* tape/guide and other items for bass (Bass Video Course etc.) are doing well (see website). Outside of that, I'm just a "lazy senior citizen" (smile).

CC: What words of advice would you give anyone starting out in music, specifically in jazz.

CK: Get your chordal note and progression skills up...don't concentrate on scale notes so much. Practice a lot, but not to the point where you bore yourself into being a "robot" on your instrument. Play your feelings always; have a GREAT sense of time (chording as well as soloing). And for heaven's sakes get your comping sense together. That's critical....the nuances of feeling like you're a horn section accenting things, not chug chug chug chug, yet stay out of the piano player's way. And please learn the finer jazz sub patterns and how to get your fluency together to play the tune, not just to show off. As the fine jazz pianist George Gaffney once said "have respect for the song;" that about says it. Avoid the "image" aspect that's a Hollywood-produced false thing. Don't do drugs either, you're just fooling yourself with that. Music is real although sometimes you have to educate the public to listen, away from the usual "visual" thing (remember, most these days were raised on "visual TV", they have to cultivate their ears more).

Loving to play music and feeling the beauty of music is a lifelong passion and playing together with other fine musicians should always be the goal. The rest always comes if you have your skills together and your heart in the right place.

Young Carol playing her prized Epiphone guitar.

Carol and Charles first meeting at the
1998 California NAMM Show.

Carol in the LA studio sometime during the 1960s.

Photo by Donna Chapman

Charles and Carol performing at the 2001 California NAMM Show.

Steve Khan – (March 1994)

Photo by David Tan

Steve Khan has released fourteen albums under his own name and has recorded with countless artists from Steely Dan to Miles Davis. As a sought-after producer, Steve's credits include albums by Mike Stern, Birelli Lagrene and Bill Connors. He has authored three books: *The Guitar Folio, Pat Martino Jazz Guitar Solos-The Early Years* and The Guitar Workshop series. In the spring semester 1994 Berklee College of Music invited Steve to be an Artist-In-Residence, where his weekly schedule included masterclasses, ensembles, career counseling and private lessons. The following interview took place on March 2, 1994 at Berklee College in Boston.

Charles Chapman: Who were some of your early influences?

Steve Khan: My early influences were B.B. King, Albert King and Freddie King; then I discovered Wes Montgomery. The way I discovered Wes was somewhat strange and quite by accident. I initially bought a record of his because I thought the guitar on the cover was the same model as B.B. King's, so I figured he must play the same kind of music. It wasn't the same guitar, the music wasn't the same, but the record truly changed my life. From there I migrated to Kenny

Burrel, Grant Green and the whole world of jazz started to open up. I began buying records by the label, *Blue Note*, etc. This exposed me to Herbie Hancock, Joe Henderson, Wayne Shorter and all the other heroes like, Miles, Trane, Sonny, etc. I think if I had to choose my four major influences on guitar it would be Kenny Burrell, Grant Green, Jim Hall and Wes Montgomery.

CC: With the clinics you have presented at colleges and schools what observations have you made?

SK: I'm overwhelmed at their work ethic and how well prepared they are. The harmonic and theoretical information they've accumulated is impressive and inspiring.

CC: What guitars do you play and what is your basic equipment setup?

SK: Since 1981 I've played mainly a Gibson ES 335 and consider this my main instrument, even though I own a few others. I still occasionally use a 1963 Fender Strat, a Charvel, and a custom ESP which I play through two large Marshal cabinets powered by two Pearce amps. I have a huge Bradshaw rack that's as big as a refrigerator and generally only use it for recordings—you cannot afford to take something like that on the road. Only a rock band that has their equipment shipped by truck can afford to use that type of equipment. The rack was originally purchased to use with Joe Zawinul's *Weather Update*. I thought it was a good investment because I had intentions of being with the band for at least five years. Unfortunately, *Weather Update* only made it through one seven-week tour and I haven't really had much use for it since. I'm currently only using a small Ibanez effects box—that's all I really need.

CC: How did you get involved in producing albums for other artists, and do you enjoy it?

SK: Most of my producing has been for other guitar players. It came about fundamentally because they like the sound of my records. I'm not talking about the sound of my guitar, I'm speaking more of the design of the total music, or how the music comes at you.

CC: So the artists have asked you to produce them, it was not something you sought out?

SK: Yes, that is right. You see, producing is very subjective, you only have your ears and your instincts. Even though you are the producer, the artist always has the last word. In two records with Mike Stern I've only won two disagreements with him. Mike knows what he wants, which is the way it should be. The down side of producing is that as an artist why do I want to spend a day, a week or a month worrying about somebody else's music? When you look at it in the hardest terms, producing takes you away from your own music. When you're working with someone the caliber of Mike Stern, and are immersed in his music for weeks on end, you're taking in influences that you may not want to have.

CC: I enjoyed your album *Let's Call This*, especially the way you and Ron Carter worked together. Did you enjoy working with Ron, and do you have any upcoming projects with him?

SK: I've worked with Ron many times as a sideman and have always enjoyed his playing. He plays on six tunes on my newest release *Headline*. Ron is a great player and the only problem I've had is that he is very particular about volume. I remember the first rehearsal for *Let's Call This*, he immediately complained about my volume. Expecting this reaction I was ALREADY playing much softer than I normally would. This situation was very difficult because I like to play loud, even though I would not be considered loud in relation to guitarists like Allan Holdsworth or Eddie Van Halen. I don't think jazz is any less physical music than rock, and to me it is every bit as intense. Not being able to play the music at the level I heard it was very tough for me.

CC: What future plans do you have?

SK: I will be recording a new CD for Polygram/Verve, *Crossings* featuring Anthony Jackson, Dennis Chambers, Maholo Badrena and Michael Brecker. I also just finished assembling *Steve Khan The Collection* for Sony Music/Columbia Contemporary Jazz Master Series. This features selections from *Tightrope* ('77), *The Blue Man* ('78), and *Arrows* ('79). In the near future I will also be on a European Tour with Anthony Jackson and Dennis Chambers.

CC: What advice would you give a guitarist who's attempting to make a living in music?

SK: A few things come to mind. First try to gather as much theoretical and technical knowledge as possible. Try to master the keyboard as a second instrument, and understand synthesis as much as you can. Make sure you have a computer, and definitely get all the knowledge about sequencing and other music based computer technology you can. Use a computer that is standard in the industry and learn all the pertinent software that goes with that system. As sad as it may be, less and less live music is being used; and if you want to make it in the business I'm afraid, at this point in time, you have to have this knowledge. One has to be prepared to expect that their dream may not pan out exactly as anticipated.

Wayne Krantz – (April 1998)

From Steely Dan sideman, to college clinician, to webmeister, this polyrhythmic fusion burner keeps his creativity and verve for playing alive.

Wayne was born on July 26, 1956 in Corvallis, OR. and after graduating from high school attended Berklee College, Boston, MA. In the Summer of 1986 he toured with Carla Bley's band and in 1991 released his first album as leader, *Signals*. Since that time Wayne has toured and worked as a clinician throughout Europe, Asia and Scandinavia besides appearing as a sideman on too many albums to list. He released a duo album with Leni Stern, *Separate Cages* and two more as leader, *Long To Be Lose* and *Two Drink Minimum*. Wayne was the guitarist for the 1996 Steely Dan tour traveling extensively throughout the United States, Europe and Japan. Last November he began working on the first Steely Dan studio album in twenty years. Wayne speaks candidly about the fairy tale manner in which he initially landed the Steely Dan gig, his touring experiences, their new album, and life after the 'Dan:'

"They were looking for a guitarist so they went out and bought a bunch of records. They had picked up my album *Long To Be Loose* and liked what they heard. Based on that album they set up an audition in LA. I flew out and played with them for a day and got the gig—it was as simple as that. There was no hype or bullshit, I didn't even know they were looking for anyone. Nobody was selling me to them, it was just on the basis of my music. I couldn't believe my luck to get that gig, but I was a bit apprehensive about it. The caliber of guitarists that have historically played with the band, puts a lot of pressure on you to perform beyond what you thought possible. Even though I felt incredible pressure throughout the tour, it was exciting and tremendous fun. The huge stages, thousands of people going nuts and excellent musicians playing great tunes. I got to solo on just about every tune and also got paid very well. I finished their '96 tour and in November '97 got the call to work on their first studio album in twenty years. It was exciting and flattering to be included in it. I worked on basic rhythm tracks for almost a month. The label will be Warner Bros; but the release date, title, duration of recording and even whether I will actually end up on the finished product are all unknown. They're perfectionists and do not release anything until they're ready. All I do know is that when it comes out it's going to be great."

Wayne is one of those guitarslingers who relies on the tone from his hands and the groove from his soul more than experimenting with refrigerator racks of equipment and dozens of guitars. He has been using the same basic setup for a number of years now: A '73 Strat through a '64 Fender Deluxe (not a Deluxe Reverb, just a Deluxe), an Alesis Microverb used as a pre-amp/gain stage, a Super Overdrive, wah-pedal occasionally and rarely, but sometimes chorus and delay. He stated "This is what I've used almost exclusively for the last four years. I find that keeping my gear basic is what works the best for me. This is the same setup I used on the 'Dan' tour, except I added a Boogie to thicken my sound. My setup looked a little ludicrous next to Walter's (Becker) kick-ass rig so I felt I had to beef mine up a bit."

When asked about future projects as well as future involvement with Steely Dan, Wayne stated "This summer I will be performing at the Edinburgh Jazz Festival in Scotland and the Brecon Festival in Wales. In November plan on a larger European tour to promote my new album *Greenwich Mean*. I am also very excited about my new website: MONSTA.com, which features new music I uploaded from my live NY shows. As I said before, the Steely Dan gig is still a mystery. Who knows when it is coming out, but I hope a few of the multitudes of rhythm tracks I recorded will make it. As far as future involvement with them—time will tell."

Tim May – (October 2000)

In the annals of studio guitarists there are really only a few that stand out in my mind: Tommy Tedesco, Howard Roberts, Bucky Pizzarelli, Tony Mottola, Mitch Holder, and Tim May. If you are not familiar with these names it wouldn't surprise me; but I guarantee you are familiar with their sound. These gentlemen are the cream of the crop and are definitely the unsung heroes of the music industry.

As one of the "first call" L.A. studio guitar players, Tim May has worked on recordings with: Celine Dion, Baby Face, Barbara Streisand, Frank Sinatra, the Pointer Sisters, Ray Charles, Patrice Rushen, Toni Braxton, John Williams, Michael Feinstein, Regina Bell, Jerry Lee Lewis, Arturo Sandoval, Les McCann, Debra Harry, David Foster, Herb Albert, Whitney Houston, George Benson, Johnny Mathis, Eddie Rabbitt, Randy Crawford, Tom Jones, Donna Summer, Amy Grant, Carol Bayer Sager, Leon Redbone, Peabo Bryson, Kenny Rogers, Dolly Parton, Janet Jackson, Quincy Jones, the Carpenters, Stan Getz, Lalo Shiffren, Al Sylvestri, Lionel Richie, Cher, Tiffany, Bill Medly, Pat Williams, Linda Ronstadt, James Horner, Smokey Robinson, Temptations, Louie Belson, Gladys Knight...you name it! Additionally, he has performed on hundreds of TV and radio commercials as well as motion pictures and television shows including: *Back to the Future*,

Practical Magic, Austin Powers, Amistad, Forrest Gump, Melrose Place, Simpsons, Family Guy, Beverly Hills 90210, King of the Hill, and *Dawson 's Creek.* He also composed and performed the score for the movie Neon Signs.

Tim was presented with the "Most Valuable Player" award from NARAS (National Academy of Recording Arts and Sciences) four years in a row and was voted into *Tune-Up Guitar* magazine's Hall of Fame in 1998. I had the honor of sharing a concert with Tim May at the 2000 NAMM show and found him to be a friendly, outgoing professional who graciously agreed to take time out of his busy schedule to share his thoughts on music, the industry, and a little of his personal history.

Charles Chapman: As with most studio players your name is never in the limelight so consequently many readers may not be familiar with your background. Please fill us in on a little of your early history.

Tim May: I was fortunate to be born into a musical family (in Cleveland, Ohio in 1953). My father Tony played bass primarily, but also played piano, sax, clarinet, and flute. My uncle, Frank May, played in the Cleveland Orchestra for 40 years. This was a tremendous help, not only for what I could learn from him, but for the total support I received in seeking a career in music! I started piano lessons when I was eight, but I really wanted to play guitar, so my dad hooked me up with a great teacher (Carl Poliafico) and I started guitar lessons. I loved it, and soon started various garage bands, and played "Battle of the Bands," etc.

My father took me to a NAMM show, and I met Bruce Bolen who is now with Fender (We have been friends ever since). Bruce was very encouraging, and he told me about Johnny Smith holding a guitar clinic in Colorado Springs. I was only 15 years old, but my parents let me fly there to attend. That is the kind of support I'll always cherish. It was an incredible event, and it was there I met Howard Roberts and Dr. William Fowler, who headed the jazz department at the University of Utah (where I ultimately went to college). I went to Howard Roberts' clinic the following year. In the meantime, I was always working lots of casuals-weddings, clubs, etc. and the occasional recording session, or show. All that was extremely educational.

As far as getting into music, it happened so early, I don't think I ever entertained the idea of doing anything else. When I was about fourteen, I knew I wanted to be a professional guitar player. When I attended Howard's seminar, he let me come along the following week to see a recording session in Hollywood. Well, that was all I needed. I knew this was for me. I'll always remember the advice Howard Roberts gave me when I told him I wanted to do session work. He said, "Move to LA when you are 20 years old. No sooner and no later." Well, I don't know if he realized how valuable that advice was. I did just that, and looking back, it was the perfect age. I was old enough to take care of myself pretty well, yet young enough not to be totally overwhelmed by how difficult it was going to be to get started!

CC: Who or what inspired you to play guitar?

TM: As far as players, I listened to lots of different kinds of music, and the guitar was involved in almost all of them. I also enjoyed listening to piano players - Chick Corea, Herbie Hanock, Keith Jarrett. I love a lot of guitar players for a lot of different reasons, but I would say early on it was Howard Roberts who really gave me that "rush" the first time I heard him. He played great, and was a wonderful influence on quite a few guitar players. Wes Montgomery, Joe Pass and George Benson were big influences too. I'll never forget when I was in high school George Benson came to Cleveland with an organ trio and burned. I went about 40 miles round trip to see him every night, and on Saturday he invited me to hang with him at the hotel. I'm sure the last thing anyone on the road would want to do is jam with a 16-year-old kid, but George and I actually sat and played together for a few hours! I was totally knocked out - what a generous thing to do - and I'll always remember that George! I find guitar players generally to be helpful and supportive of one another.

CC: How does studio work differ now compared to ten or fifteen years ago?

TM: Studio work is not that different than it was when I started (I moved to L.A. in 1974). I believe there was more work then because most sessions had two, and sometimes three guitars and there

was more live rhythm tracking - but that seems to be the main difference. That makes it tougher than ever to break in, but I still think guys that can play will get a shot. It just means there are fewer times when someone has to try a new guitar player because everyone else is busy. But the fundamental gig is the same. It's always a different situation, and often times adaptability is the key. There are many more "home studios" than before, and some very good ones. Eddie Arkin composed the score for Melrose Place for a number of years, and has a great studio, and it was a total pleasure to work there and be able to totally focus on the guitar. Sometimes the home studios have limitations that guitar players have to deal with to get the right sound. Again, it's a matter of adaptability.

CC: With your extensive studio career, does any particular session stick out in your mind?

TM: I think the most memorable sessions for me were the ones where some player played an "incredible something" that knocked everyone out. I heard Tom Tedesco play some things on film sessions that made me cry they were so lovely. Once on a Lalo Shiffrin date, there were two or three of us "hot guys" playing all day, and Tedesco was sleeping on the couch. Then late in the session they woke up Tom to play his part. He wiped his face with his hand and sat down in front of a 4-5 page nylon guitar solo, all alone with Lalo conducting, and the entire orchestra sitting all around the Warner Brothers scoring stage. Well, the red light went on and he just nailed it the first time. The rest of us guitar players got a real good guitar lesson that day. He was a brilliant guitarist and is sorely missed in this business. I think playing with some of the incredible musicians I've had the opportunity to play with is the biggest thrill for me.

CC: What guitar or guitars do you consider you mainstay instruments?

TM: The mainstays for me are a John Carruthers custom "Strat" type electric with Floyd Rose tremolo (very versatile) a Martin D-18 flat-top (early '60's) a Yamaha nylon-string (one of two high-end prototypes made in 1980; Lee Ritenour has the sister guitar), a big Guild 12-string flat-top and a Guild "Artist Award" archtop electric or jazz and acoustic. I also frequently substitute a Tele or a 335 or Les Paul for the electric. After that, there are all the Dobros, banjos, mandolins, lap steels, Weisenborns,

Rickenbacker 12s, bass guitars, sitars, tiples, high-string and all the ethnic stuff like balalaikas, bazoukis, etc. The list is pretty long, but the "staples" are what I mentioned in the first paragraph.

CC: What is your live rig like and how does that differ in the studio?

TM: My live rig is an Egnater pre-amp into an old Benson power amp. I also use a Rane parametric EQ, and a Master Room Reverb. A 15" early '70s vintage Altec-Lansing and sometimes a 12" same vintage Altec-Lansing extension cabinet. My session rig is a rack with an Egnater pre-amp and a Rivera M-1 amp with the Egnater and the Rivera I have six pre-amps to choose from. I also have an Eventide processor, a DBX limiter, a Korg delay, a Roland processor, a Cry-Baby, and a Roland volume pedal. I run this through a Rocktron patch bay and Ground Control controller set up by Ralph Skelton at Pacific Innovative Electronics. I use two, 12" Rivera speaker cabs.

CC: Have you ever owned or do you still own any guitars that you feel are memorable?

TM: I own some wonderful guitars, some more "vintage or collectable" than others, but the most unique one might be a Gibson that my friend Mitch Holder got them to make back in the early 80s. It's one of 10 or 12 from the factory, like a 355 with three single coils. Blond, and a real beauty! I have been playing Guild's "Artist Award" guitar for my jazz performances. I found a real good one in 1980, and the new one seems like a great instrument. Bob Benedetto did some real nice things to the instrument. Other than that I think I probably own at least one of every major brand of guitar made.

CC: What strings, picks or any other accessories do you use?

TM: I like the Fender extra heavy teardrop picks, and Guild strings work well. I use generally 9s on my Strats, and Teles, and a pretty heavy (15s-56s) on my Arch top electric. I also use D'Addario, SIT, and John Pearse from time to time. I use Shubb capos and various kinds of slides.

CC: What advice would you give a young guitarist wanting to make a career in music, particularly as a studio musician?

TM: For players wanting to get involved in session work, it's all word of mouth. I think that is the same as when I started-one guy likes the way you play, and mentions it to another player, who recommends you to someone else and on and on. So each time you play, you build that.

I remember when I first moved to town, I would work with anybody once. One more guy will know your capabilities and if the gig stinks, you don't go back - but it could turn into a great gig. One of my very first gigs was when Freddie Tacket asked me to sub for him in a John Davidson impersonator show! I did it and it was pretty dumb, but I met five guys I didn't know before! Plus learned to read music! For most of the mainstream session work, especially TV and movies, you have to read - that's all there is to it! You never will get the chance to show off your totally new and exiting solo style if you can't also do the other stuff that requires reading. The more you can do as a musician, the more work is available to you. Professionalism is a must. Good equipment, attitude - it all helps. I hate to see good players not work as much as they would like because of a goofy reason like reliability problems! However, session work is not for everyone. I can really understand how some musicians are only interested in playing what they want to play, when they want to do it.

I'm still doing my session thing in L.A. and I really still dig it. As guitarists, we are in all styles of music, and probably allowed more personal "input" in the parts we play, and I love the variety. From "There's no chart, and we don't know what we want" to "this chord solo has to be rendered exactly as written and played with a 90-piece orchestra," and everything in between. I also love the idea of rehearsing a piece of music until it sounds really good, recording it, then moving on and not playing it again! In my group, spontaneity is very important. We never play anything the same way twice!

CC: Could you fill us in on upcoming projects, gigs, etc.?

TM: The new thing for me is playing live in L.A. with my group. I've been writing forever, and it's fun to get the music played. We have been playing a great jazz club here called Rocco's, and a few others. Abe Laboriel, Ray Pizzi, Mike Lang, and Bob Zimmitti, and I have been playing my original stuff and it's been lots of fun. I released my first solo album *One Piece of the Big Picture* on Miramar Records last year, (available at many record stores, and on-line from CD NOW and Amazon.com) and we started playing around town after that. It's been something I kind of didn't do much of for a number of years and feels great to get back into it!

I will be putting together a website that I hope to get up and running very soon. In the meantime I can be contacted at mayzing@aol.com. I have a good catalog of solo guitar pieces with music and tab, some ensemble recordings and quite a bit of educational material that really focuses on every aspect of professional guitar playing- styles, technique, reading, improvising, studio work; the real "working guitar player in the real world" kind of instruction. The Internet is a great way to communicate. I also am planning on-line seminars, and one-on-one instruction in the near future.

Tim in the studio

California NAMM 2000 concert. Photo by Donna Chapman
(Back row, left to right) Tim May, Randy Johnston, Howard Alden, Johnny Smith,
Jimmy Bruno, Bob Benedetto, Dan Faehnle, Charles Chapman, Kenny Burrell,
Bill Doyle, and Randall Kremer of the Smithsonian Institution.
(Front row, left to right) Fender CEO Bill Schultz, Bruce Bolen, Ken Wild,
Bob Heinrich, and Cindy Benedetto.

Vinnie Moore — *(November 1997)*

Photo by Michelle Morton

Vinnie Moore began playing guitar at age 12. After many years of clubs and small venues he finally caught national attention via *Guitar Player Magazine's* "Spotlight" column. Shortly thereafter, the Delaware native was contracted by Pepsi-Cola for a musical sound byte that had Moore's playing blow the caps off Pepsi bottles. It later became the first ever western commercial to be televised in the Soviet Union. Moore has recorded four solo albums. His first, *Mind's Eye*, was released in 1987 selling over 100,000 copies. It also received the prestigious "Best New Talent" honors in both *Guitar Player* and *Guitar World* magazines. His next three albums received similar accolades in addition to selling in the six figures. He was a member of Alice Cooper's band, and is an international solo performing artist. Vinnie has conducted over 150 clinics and has released two instructional videos that have sold over 25,000 copies.

Charles Chapman: Who were your early musical influences?

Vinnie Moore: There were tons of them: Ritchie Blackmore, Brian May, Jeff Beck, Van Halen, Robin Trower. After I played for a few years it turned into more fusion type guys like Al DiMeola, Larry Carlton, Dave Gilmore, Hendrix, Santana—I could go on and on.

CC: Your first two solo albums *Minds Eye* and *Time Odyssey* were comprised mostly of neo-classical compositions. What influenced you to write in that genre?

VM: I was listening to Bach, Handel and a lot of Baroque composers at that time and it really had a direct influence on my song writing.

CC: Your newer material seems to be more blues/fusion oriented than the neo-classical older material. Is that something you were intentionally striving for or did it just evolve?

VM: It just evolved. I never intentionally or consciously tried to do anything in particular. I just picked up the guitar and let the creativity take me wherever it wanted to go. Around the time I finished recording my second album *Time Odyssey* I burned out on the classical stuff. That happens with me a lot. I get sick of doing the same things and then I have to start fresh with another approach or I will get bored.

CC: With regard to your virtuosic solos on songs such as *In Control, Hero Without Honor,* and *Meltdown;* how did you develop such speed and accuracy on the guitar?

VM: Lots of practicing and breaking things down into exercises; like alternate picking chromatic exercises, left hand strength and coordination exercises, etc. Having a strong focus and direction, with a daily practice routine is usually the answer. There is no easy way, it just takes a lot of hard work.

CC: On your second video you were in the middle of a solo when you shut off the distortion and went into a very jazz oriented chord progression and then did a short solo in the same style. Have you studied jazz and do plan to do any jazz type tunes in up coming projects?

VM: The piece you mention was completely improvised on the spot and I honestly can't remember exactly what I did. Growing up I studied with a guitar teacher outside of Philadelphia, Nick Bucci, who studied with Pat Martino. He turned me on to Pat Martino, Joe Pass, Pat Metheny and many other jazz guitarists. I think it influenced my phrasing, and people often tell me they can hear a little jazz in my solos. In the future I may record something with a jazzy groove, but I would not be comfortable actually trying to play jazz.

CC: What was it like working with Alice Cooper on the "Operation Rock & Roll" Tour in 1991?

VM: That was a very good experience for me. I had been a solo artist for most of the time up to that point, and it was nice to go out and not have the weight of the world on my shoulders. It was a fun gig that I really enjoyed. It wasn't the type of thing I would want to do forever, but it was definitely a good experience.

CC: Are there any guitarists today that you admire or listen too?

VM: I still like to listen to my old favorites, but guitarists like Allan Holdsworth, Steve Morse, Strunz and Farah are also incredible and are among my favorites.

CC: Can you tell us about any upcoming projects?

VM: I'm leaving for Italy tomorrow to do a series of clinics, and then I intend to be in the studio shortly after the first of the year to record a new album. I have most of the tunes written and just have to write a few more and pull together some loose ends. Hopefully, it will be out in Spring of 1998.

CC: What advice could you give a guitarist about to embark on a career in music?

VM: Enjoy it and love what you're doing. Take experiences from your life and express them through your music. If you can touch a nerve in the listener, or make them feel, what you feel you've accomplished your goal. Try to use your music as an extension of who you are and have fun with it.

Music Man ad

Steve Morse – (October 1993)

Steve Morse was born in Hamilton, Ohio and stands first and foremost among rock's greatest guitar virtuosos. He is a master technician, able to execute burning single note lines and chordal passages with such speed and accuracy that he has received worldwide recognition and critical acclaim.

Steve was voted five times winner of *Guitar Player* magazines's "Best Overall Guitarist" and a member of the prestigious "Gallery of the Greats." He is best know for his performances with the Dixie Dregs, Kansas and the Steve Morse Band. He has toured with Al DiMeola, John McLaughlin, Paco DeLucia and has written music and performed on four Grammy Award Shows. Besides his virtuosity as a performer he is well respected as a writer, clinician and educator.

Charles Chapman: Who were some of your early influences?

Steve Morse: The Beatles, Rolling Stones, and more specifically Eric Clapton, Page, Hendrix, Beck and definitely John McLaughlin.

CC: Your technique is very impressive. Is this something you consciously worked on or did it develop as your musical skills matured?

SM: Technique is something you definitely have to work on. A certain amount of it can be developed by just playing the tunes, but if you want to keep that edge, and be sure that every sixteenth note is exact, you must constantly work on it.

CC: Is it difficult finding time to practice both classical and electric guitars?

SM: Definitely! You must have strong mental fortitude and energy to use every single minute of your practice time in a productive manner. I do find that the instruments complement each other and the more you practice both the easier everything gets.

CC: Do you set up a specific practice schedule for yourself?

SM: I divide my approach into two different areas. For a period of time after a tour or recording I tend to get into a less structured practice schedule focusing on a new and upcoming project.

CC: I heard a rumor that you might have a classical album coming out in the near future. Is there any truth to this?

SM: This is something I've wanted to do for a long time, but the likelihood of it happening is not in the near future. I've recently changed labels and they are not receptive to a project like this.

CC: Do you feel being left handed, and playing right handed has been an advantage or a deterrent in your playing?

SM: I've never thought about it and I do not really think it matters a lot. I must admit though that I've never had a loose right hand and I hold the pick differently than most players. I also rotate my wrist around two axes instead of one and I've always had to work on my right hand more than my left. All this may have something to do with the fact that I am left handed, but as I said before, I've never really thought that much about it.

CC: What is the most satisfying aspect of your career?

SM: The people! I approach every show with a very aggressive feeling of "I want to do this right. I want to make this thing happen." At the end of every concert I love to hang out and meet with as many fans as possible. I get so much back from them. Last night I went through a bunch of letters that I've been meaning to answer for a long time, and it was incredible how well written and thoughtful they were. I measure success I terms of what I've set out to do versus what I'm doing. I'm in this for the long term and as long as I can do what I love and make people happy, I consider myself successful and satisfied.

CC: How do approach songwriting?

SM: My approach varies, I may write from the guitar, piano, or just try to imagine it all in my mind before I set it to the instruments. I intentionally use alternate approaches to keep the songs different. My first requirement is to come up with an idea I really like, and then analyze it to make sure it isn't too much like something else. I kind of mold the general direction early on, and then let it grow at its own pace and try not to put a deadline on when it's going to be finished. I feel the ideas are free and all offer the place. The trick is to create an environment where your mind will kind of coast into the next section.

CC: What words of advice can you give a student?

SM: First imagine, even if it's only for one minute a day, what it was like when you were trying to gather the money to go to music school, buy an instrument, or just having someone support you while you're learning. Do this every day so you realize the sacrifice it's taking for you to develop your art form. I can say without exaggeration, that every morning when I sit down to breakfast I think about the people who have paid for the food I'm eating. This is a very cause and effect relationship that I do not want to see changed. Right now, if you're enjoying the opportunity to learn because of somebody else's efforts you need to acknowledge it. If you do this for a few moments every day it will help keep everything in perspective.

The next advice would be to try to apply everything you've learned. The best way to do this is by picking up the guitar and playing with other musicians as regularly as possible. The best thing I did when I was in college was the numerous impromptu, not a complete band, kind of jam where I tried to apply things I just learned. Also, remember that what you are studying does not have to be what you want to play. For example, if your teacher gives you a jazz tune to learn you shouldn't say: "Hey, I'm not into jazz, I don't want to work on this." If you want to grow, you should work on and learn all types of music. I can guarantee that it will improve your own form of music and make you a much more complete musician.

Joe Negri – *(September 1999)*

For over thirty years I have played, taught and been a strong devotee of jazz guitar. Through the years I would often get embroiled in discussions on who the great guitarists were, both past and present. The names bantered about were always Wes Montgomery, Joe Pass, Herb Ellis and Johnny Smith, but every once in a while the name of Joe Negri would come up; especially if the person speaking was from or had recently been in Pittsburgh, PA. More times than I can count I have scanned record bins trying to hunt down Joe's recordings, but to no avail. I was told that he has a long standing role as "Handyman Negri" on the PBS show *Mister Rogers' Neighborhood,* but quite frankly I have never seen the show and this was not a place I would go to search out jazz guitar talent.

Last July I finally had the opportunity to be in the Pittsburgh area and made a point of looking up this elusive jazz guitar icon. I found him to be a soft spoken man devoid of hype, egomania, and many of the characteristics that plague our industry today. Even though he is a gentleman from the "old school," when the guitar enters his hands his eyes twinkle and this seasoned professional turns into a young lion playing lines and comping chords that definitely makes you sit up and take notice.

Joe was a musical prodigy at age four, and was touring nationally with the Shep Fields Orchestra by age sixteen. He has recorded and performed extensively with such renowned performers as Johnny Mathis, Tony Bennett, Andy Williams, Wynton, Branford and Ellis Marsalis, Yo Yo Ma and Martin Taylor. Most recently he was featured with Ishtak Pearlman, John Williams and the Pittsburgh Symphony Orchestra on the highly acclaimed CD *Cinema Serenade.*

For more than twenty years Joe has served as musical director at WTAE-TV in Pittsburgh, PA. He has been a key performer on the PBS *Mister Rogers' Neighborhood* show as Handyman Negri since its inception. He has also distinguished himself as a composer teaming with humorist/writer Bob McCully writing and producing several musical reviews. In collaboration with composer Lou Tracy, Joe has written over twenty songs. His most recent work, *The Mass of Hope* (scored for mixed choir and jazz ensemble) has received critical and artistic acclaim from both press and the musical communities.

Currently Joe teaches at Pitt, Duquesne and CMU. He is credited with changing the face of plectrum guitar instruction in Pittsburgh. In the 1970s he wrote a curriculum for teaching jazz guitar that was adopted by the University of Pittsburgh and eventually Carnegie Mellon and Duquesne Universities.

While in Pittsburgh I attended a clinic Joe was presenting to music educators at Duquesne University. I was also able to hear him perform solo guitar, with a big band, and finally found his wonderful new release *Afternoon in Rio* (JAZZ MCG 1004). Since then I have corresponded and spoken with Joe on numerous occasions and with each encounter my respect grows as the realization that Joe Negri is truly one of Pittsburgh's best kept secrets.

The following was conducted at Joe's home in Pittsburgh on September 16, 1999:

Charles Chapman: Why have I had such a hard time finding recordings of yours?

Joe Negri: I've recorded quite extensively over the years, but mainly as a sideman. I did an album about twenty-five years ago and it never got beyond the Pittsburgh area. I love to record, and I'm quite comfortable in the studio. However, the "business" of recording has always, somehow eluded me. I was thrilled when Marty and Jay Ashby and the folks at the "Manchester Craftsmen's Guild" approached me with the idea of a recording project, *Afternoon In Rio*. It's now available on CD and has received very good reviews.

CC: I have heard about your penchant for practicing triad exercises up and across the fingerboard. How does this influence the way you approach comping and improvisation?

JN: Triads help me to visualize the fingerboard—they give me a kind of a vertebrae structure to build my lines on. I try to visualize major and minor sounds and then create dominant, minor and major seven sonorities from that, with my altered sounds coming from the diminished and augmented triads. I try to break everything down to a common denominator.

CC: Please elaborate on your picking style and how it effects your melodic phrasing.

JN: Alternate picking is my basic stroke, but I use down strokes for all accents and syncopations. Also for all slurs, including hammers and pull offs. I also use sweep picking quite a bit, but only sweep ascending rarely descending. Descending sweeps are much more difficult to control than the ascending sweeps. Consequently the time suffers, so as a result, I avoid them. I am basically a swing/bebop player and the element of "time" is most important to me.

CC: How did you land the long standing role as "Handyman Negri" on *Mister Rogers' Neighborhood* show?

JN: Fred Rogers is a gifted songwriter and we have been friends for many years. We originally worked together in the early days of local Pittsburgh TV. When Fred moved to PBS to start what is now known as *Mister Rogers' Neighborhood*, he asked me if I would take the role of Handyman Negri. I told him I was not very handy and he assured me I would be just fine—that was thirty-two years ago.

CC: You are very active in a program called "Jazz For Juniors" and are an advocate of bringing jazz to the ears of children. What exactly is this program?

JN: I have been involved in this for the last six years and it is an interactive program for kids from ages three to eight. I perform in a trio setting with keyboard and drums and the kids love it. The children interact by dancing and singing; and I have a little segment I call open stage, where I give them a chance to come up and sing a song. The thing that's great is all the children are so natural with a great innate sense of rhythm. They are very open to anything you present to them and have no inhibitions about performing and just enjoy themselves. I spend quite a bit of time with this program and have had great success with it. It's kind of my way to give back to society for the many blessings I've had over the years.

CC: I'm told your first meeting with Emily Remler was an unusual one. Please tell us about it.

JN: Emily was playing a date in Pittsburgh, and was scheduled to be on an early morning talk show where I was the musical director. I would accompany guest singers or instrumentalists and would also provide all the musical "in's" and "out's" for commercials, etc. Emily and I had never met, and she was very skeptical about me accompanying her. When she was told that I would back her up she stated that she really would rather play solo. I opened the show as I always did; and to my surprise Emily went running to the powers-that-be during a break, and stated that she changed her mind and really wanted to perform with me. She moved to Pittsburgh for a short while and we became quite good friends and performed together on several gigs and concerts.

CC: Have you owned any unusual guitars over the years and what equipment are you currently using?

JN: I owned a 1943 D'Angelico New Yorker non-cutaway that I played for ten or fifteen years. I now own a very nice 1969 Guild Stewart X 500 that I use occasionally on nice quiet jazz gigs, as well as a custom Heritage Golden Eagle and a Guild X170 Manhattan that is sort of my all purpose gig guitar.

I own two amplifiers, a Polytone mini brute 2 and a Walter Woods mono amp head that I play through a custom cabinet with a Mesa Boogie 12" speaker. The Polytone is my gig amp that I use for clubs and small venues. For recording and jazz concerts I always use my Woods setup. I am currently using .013 D'Addario flatwound string set with Fender oval heavy picks.

CC: What upcoming projects do you have in the works?

JN: I am very fortunate to be booked through the Fall of 2000. I'm half way through another album that I'm very excited about it—a tribute to Duke Ellington. The personnel will include: Roger Humphries, Dwayne Dolphin, Jay and Marty Ashby, Steve Rudolph, Gerry Neiwood and Mike Tomaro on reeds and flutes. With any luck it will be out early next year.

I'm also in the process of writing a book on my triad improvisation concepts. Tim Bedner, a fine guitarist and a nice guy, is helping me with this and I am very excited about getting my ideas into book format.

CC: What advice would you give a young musician embarking on a career as a guitarist?

JN: Try to seek out good people to study with and work on your reading. There is a wealth of material available today—and reading is a great asset for anyone trying to develop a jazz vocabulary. Reading will open the door to many exciting possibilities. We all have to make a living, but try not to compromise your ideals. Find you own musical voice, follow your dream, but also know your capabilities.

Joe with his 1969 Guild X500.

Photo by Donna Chapman

Jack Petersen – *(July 1997)*

Jack Petersen was born in Oklahoma shortly thereafter his family moved to Denton, Texas where he spent his formative years. He started playing guitar at age fourteen, with his initial influence being western swing. It wasn't until 1956 when he enlisted in the 8th Army Band that he became absorbed in jazz. After he left the army he attended North Texas State where he played cello and bass in the symphony orchestra, and guitar and piano in the jazz ensemble.

He has shared the stage with such luminaries as Stan Kenton, Clark Terry, Howard Roberts, Doc Severinsen and Johnny Smith to name a few. Jack has performed on countless albums and has two published texts: *Jazz Guitar Styles & Analysis* and *The Art of Improvisation Vols. I & II.*

Jack held the position of Guitar Chair at Berklee College of Music from 1962 until 1965. In addition to being one of the most in-demand studio musicians in Dallas, Texas for over a decade, he has taught at North Texas State and University of North Florida at Jacksonville.

Jack is still an active performer, clinician and teacher; residing in Sarasota, Florida where this interview took place.

Charles Chapman: You are originally from Texas, what events lead up to you becoming the Chair of the Guitar Department at Berklee?

Jack Petersen: I used to teach in the Stan Kenton jazz camps that were run by Gene Hall. These were the first summer jazz schools ever. At these camps guitarists were starting to become more prominent so I set up guitar groups to give them more performance opportunities. A number of Berklee teachers taught at these camps and were impressed at what I was doing, and recommended me for a teaching position at the school. Lawrence Berk offered me the job of setting up the fledgling Guitar Department and I thought it would be fun.

CC: When was that?

JP: That was in 1962. At that time the school was located on Newbury Street and there were only nine guitar students in the department.

CC: How long did you stay and do you remember any of your students?

JP: I stayed until 1965, John Abercrombie and Mick Goodrick were two of my first students.

CC: What are some of your most vivid memories?

JP: I remember the students were eager to learn and it was a great musical environment. The main style of music was jazz and big bands were flourishing. Everywhere you turned there was a big band rehearsing, playing great music.

CC: Why did you leave?

JP: I met my wife Claudette in Boston. In fact, she was a secretary at the school. We had a child and I wasn't sure I wanted to raise her in Boston. You have to understand that I did a lot of performing in the Dallas Fort Worth studios before I came to Boston, and I was getting a lot of calls for great work back in Texas. So after a while I just thought it would be the best for my career and my family to move back to Texas.

CC: When did you start teaching at North Texas State?

JP: Gene Hall had set up a very good jazz department at North Texas that was continuing to grow and attract many guitarists. Berklee and the North Texas jazz programs started at the same time. Musicians were getting out of the army and wanted to learn how to write for dance bands so they could make a living. Berklee and North Texas were among the few that could offer them the skills they needed. Very few people knew how to write well for big bands and you could make a good living doing it. The GI Bill would pay their college tuition and it was a good deal. Over the years I kept getting offers to teach, but I was so busy in the studio that I did not have the time. In 1975 Gene asked me one more time and then I felt the time was right.

CC: You then went on teach at the University of North Florida in Jacksonville. How did that come about?

JP: I had been teaching at North Texas for twelve years when a good friend of mine, Rich Matteson, asked me if I would be interested in joining him in Florida. I had taught with Rich at North Texas and once again I felt the timing was right.

CC: What guitars and amplifiers do you use?

JP: I have a Benedetto Fratello, a Fender D'Aquisto and believe it or not a Fender Stratocaster. The Benedetto is my favorite, in fact, I've owned many guitars including a few D'Angelicos and nothing comes close to the Benedetto. For amplifiers I have a Yamaha, a Fender, and two Polytones, the Mini-Brute II as well as the next larger model.

CC: I just heard that you will be a guest at the Berklee Guitar Summer Sessions this upcoming August. What will your schedule be like and what will your main focus be with the students?

JP: I am going to teach what I call the mechanics of the neck, where we build chords from theory, not chord diagrams or tablature. I don't have a problem if students use these as tools, but there comes a time when you just have to know the notes that are in your chords and how they correspond on the neck. I will probably be teaching improvisation and also be performing in clinics and concerts.

CC: What advice could you give a student starting out?

JP: In the beginning stages don't worry about money, play for the love of it, give it everything you can. There is nothing wrong with focusing on one style of music, but keep your eyes open and see what's out there. Listen to all kinds of music. People are always shocked at my record collection. I have John Abercrombie, John Scofield, Mike Stern, Bill Frisell, Jeff Beck and too many more to name. I just love all kinds of music. I'm 63 and I love to play more now than I did when I was younger.

Jack at Berklee in the 1960's.

Bucky Pizzarelli – (April 2000)

John (Bucky) Pizzarelli was born on January 9, 1926 in Paterson, NJ. His father enamored with everything western and cowboys gave him the moniker of Buckskin. Bucky, as he became known, was fascinated by the music always present at family gatherings. His maternal uncles, Pete and Bobby Domenick were professionals of the day and taught their very exuberant nephew the basics of banjo and guitar. They instilled in him the love of music and the joy of sharing that he continues to nurture with his family and audiences all over the world.

To quote from Mel Bay's *Master Anthology of Jazz Guitar Solos, Volume One* (formerly *2000 Jazz Guitar*) book: "Bucky Pizzarelli is an international renowned man of music. His instrument of choice is the guitar, and his style is jazz. For more a than a half a century he has been a part of the fraternity of musicians who have kept the mainstream and traditional jazz alive."

Bucky has been, and still is, one of the busiest and most recorded guitarists in the annals of jazz guitar history. His name is not commonplace, but it's highly unlikely that you haven't heard his music. In the late 1960s he starting playing the 7-string guitar becoming the "pied piper" for the burgeoning instrument. Most of the young lions of this instrument site Bucky as their main influence. Jazz guitarists: Howard Alden, Jimmy Bruno, Ron Eschete, Andy MacKenzie, Jerry Sims and John Pizzarelli Jr. are just a few of his staunchest admirers.

The association with George Barnes in 1969 earned him critical and public acclaim in a duo that still sets the standard for this jazz guitar genre. His son John is carrying on the tradition with a groove and swing that just won't quit. When I asked John how he developed his great swing feel he stated: "Growing up in my house, if you couldn't swing you weren't allowed at the dinner table."

The list of musicians Bucky has performed with is the veritable "Who's Who" of music history and is too long to even start to list. In the 1970s a young up and coming guitar maker, Robert Benedetto, walked into a Florida lounge and heard a sound that drew him to the music and the musician. They immediately had a rapport both musically and personally, that formed an alliance which has passed the test of time. In many circles the name Bucky Pizzarelli is synonymous not only with great jazz, but the 7-string guitar, and the world famous Benedetto archtops. He became the first major endorser for Benedetto guitars and still to date considers these fine instruments an integral part of his sound.

Bob Benedetto states:
"Bucky Pizzarelli is widely regarded for his tasteful and uncluttered playing style. He is the gentleman of the legitimate guitar, respected as both a great musician and a fine human being.

He became my first well-known endorser. Since that time, we have maintained a special friendship; he's responsible for many who play Benedetto guitars!

As affirmed by countless musicians, he is an absolute pleasure to play with as both soloist and accompanist. Credited for popularizing the 7-string guitar, his influence is vast. Bucky's seemingly endless energy has propelled him through over five and a half decades as a premier player. Always in demand, he continues to perform worldwide, content to do what he does best."

The following interview was conducted at Bucky's home in New Jersey on April 30, 2000.

Charles Chapman: When did you join NBC and how long were you with them?

BP: After I was discharged from the army I immediately went on the road with the Vaughn Monroe Band. I was with them for about six years when I received a call from NBC—that was in 1953. They asked if I would be interested in being the guitar player for the *Kate Smith Show* and I jumped at it so I could get back to NYC on a permanent basis. It was broadcast live with lots of guests that covered much more ground than the shows do today—a true variety show. Anyone with any kind of fame or notoriety from politicians, movie stars, famous musicians of the day all came on the show. This was a Monday through Friday commitment, and NBC would also have you do small radio shows at night. Radio was very big during that time with all the shows having live bands. In fact, a Saturday night radio show called the *Hit Parade* had one of the largest groups I ever saw directed by Raymond Scott. It had a huge brass section, strings and George Barnes was often the guitarist. They played all the hits of the day and it was tremendous. I stayed with NBC for about three years full time and was on staff basis for many years after that.

CC: What exactly does "staff basis" mean.

BP: That meant I was on an "as needed" basis and paid by the job. This proved to be advantageous because as soon as The Three Suns heard I was no longer full time with NBC they asked me to join them.

CC: Who were the Three Suns?

BP: They were a very popular group comprised of organ, accordion and guitar. They were often featured with the Vaughn Monroe band when I was with them. When their guitarist, Al Nevins, had a heart attack and couldn't play anymore they gave me a call, and I was on the road with them for almost two years. They wore white tuxedos and all the instruments were white: the organ, the accordion and they even supplied me with a white guitar. Believe it or not it was a D'Angelico.

CC: That's unbelievable!

BP: They actually had two on the truck. A big 18" and the 16" and I had my choice. I preferred the 16" and always played that one.

CC: Do you know what ever happened to it?

BP: Sure, I own it. After I had played with them for a while they bought another white guitar similar to a Les Paul, but hollow, and told me I could keep the 16" D'Angelico. I took it back to John (D'Angelico) and had him strip it down. He left it natural and it is a real beauty. In fact, I used it last week when I played with Michael Feinstein.

CC: You mentioned George Barnes, how did the duo start?

BP: I had known of George for many years and he was one of my favorite guitar players. He was quite famous from the time he was sixteen or seventeen. He was from Chicago and I originally met him when we shared recording sessions in NY. We hit it off both musically and personally and always enjoyed each others company. The duo was actually formed in 1969 and we achieved great critical acclaim. We played Carnegie Hall, featured on the Carson show and had a steady gig at the St. Regis where many famous people used to come to hear us. We played on a regular basis for about three years.

CC: How many albums did you do with George and why did it come to a close?

BP: We only made two or three albums. Everybody loved us, but we still had trouble getting good work for good money. Rock and roll was selling the records and we just couldn't make a living with the duo.

CC: Two musicians you've worked with over the years I know our readers would like to hear about, Benny Goodman and Stephane Grappelli. Please tell us how you met them, how long you performed with them, etc.?

BP: I first met Benny in 1958 when he was featured on a show sponsored by Texaco. I was in the studio band directed by Ralph Burns and Benny commented that he liked the way I played. The next time we met was when he was a guest on the Carson show where I was in the house band with Skitch Henderson. A little while after that he called and asked me to do four weeks with him at the Waldorf Astoria Hotel. It was perfect. I would get done recording the Carson show about 7 or 8 and run over to the Waldorf and do the gig with Benny. I did four very large European tours and performed with him sporadically the rest of his life. The last gig I did with him was about two years before he died—he was still playing magnificently!

I first met Stephane Grappelli when I received a call to play with the Boston POPS Orchestra. They were doing a salute to Eddie Lang and Joe Venuti and Stephane Grappelli was being featured. They needed a guitarist who knew the style of Lang so they called me to come to Boston to do the show. A little while later I was asked to play a jazz festival in Nice, France and I had no idea who I was going to play with. When you're hired to play festivals you never know who they are going to pair you up with.

CC: Some things never change!

BP: (Laughs) You're so right on that one. Anyway, when I arrived George Wein (festival organizer) came up to me and said: "Go to stage 3". When I arrived at Stage #3 it was outside and Stephane Grappelli was there waiting for me, and there were also people there to record it. We had no music or set arrangement we just called tunes and played. We played for three or four hours and a record was actually made from it. It was titled *Duet with Stephane Grappelli* (Blue and Black label).

I played with Stephane too many times to remember, but mainly in the United States. We performed a few times at the Umbria Jazz Festival in Italy, but I was mainly called when he toured in the States. I played with him right up until he died and have nothing but great memories. We all knew and liked the same tunes and he loved the music so much it was always a thrill to work with him.

CC: A while back you told me a very funny story about a green Gretch guitar that you once owned. How did it go?

BP: Fred Gretch was a big fan of the duo with George Barnes. He used to be a regular at our St. Regis gig and was a delightful gentleman. He invited us to the factory and told use he would make us anything we wanted. I owned a George Van Eps 7-string model and I told him I wanted everything simplified. One pickup, two knobs, and I told him

to make it the same color as George's. I had no idea what color it was until I got it and it was green. It was a very good guitar and I used it a lot. The pickup was pushed in a few years later by the airlines and I took it to Pasquale across from Sam Ash Music to get it repaired. I was really tired of the color so I told him to paint it brown while he was repairing it. Once I received my Benedetto 7-string that was all I used on gigs, and put the Gretch on my sun porch to have something to practice on when I was out there. During certain times of the day the sun would shine on the guitar and it must have brought the original color out, because the green started to come through. Before long it was back to the original color.

CC: Sounds to me like it was haunted. Do you still own it?

BP: No, I gave it to the University of Illinois where Rick Hayden is.

CC: Is the Benedetto your main guitar and how many do you own?

BP: Oh yes, the Benedetto is my main instrument and it is the guitar I use 99% of the time. Occasionally I will pull the D'Angelico out, because I really do like the way it sounds with a big band, but that's very rare. Bob has made four 7-string archtops for me. The first in 1978, the second in 1981, the third in 1990 and the last one in 1998. All four are sunbursts. The first three have 17" body widths and the most recent a 16". I have been with Bob for many years and his guitars just play and sound great.

CC: Tell us how you became enamored with the 7-string guitar?

BP: I first heard the 7-string in 1969 when George Van Eps was in New York demonstrating his new 7-string Gretch model. It just made sense and I could never figure out why it didn't catch on. There is nothing like the seven-string when you are playing rhythm. You're not stuck for notes, everything is right under your hands without jumping around. The beauty of the 7-string is not the low notes, but when you are playing high up on the neck and need a nice note—there it is. The 7-string is the instrument of the future and I predict that most guitarists of stature, in any style, will be playing on the 7-string guitar in the next ten years.

CC: What amps, strings, etc., do you prefer?

BP: I really don't have a preference in amps. One is usually provided wherever I perform, and I've learned to get an acceptable sound from any good quality amp. I only use the LaBella #800-7 black taped strings. I've tried many others, but I immediately come back to those.

CC: You still tour extensively. How do cope with the rigors of being on the road? Do you still enjoy it or is it just part of the job?

BP: You see, it's not just a job, it's my life and part of me. The material is what keeps it interesting and fun. When I'm on the road I'm always thinking about what tunes I'm going to present and how I'm going to play them. I don't want to keep playing the same tunes night after night. I like looking for obscure underground tunes or new songs that will work with my style or the other musicians I'm performing with. I work very hard at what I do and take pride in it. This also keeps the music fresh and makes the time go by quickly. When I have control of the situation, I don't mind traveling. As long I know where I'm going, who I'm playing with and the type of venue—it's still great fun!

CC: What do you do to relax when you are not on the road?

BP: I love to play golf and paint. Also, when I'm not traveling I like to spend as much time as I can with my family.

CC: So many musicians, especially touring musicians, personal lives are a wreak. How have you been able to maintain such a stable family life?

BP: I was always taught to dress up when you appear in front of people. Respect the music and always play to the best of your ability and people will respect you. I have always been very close with my family and they have always been there for me and hopefully I have for them as well. My family is my lifeline, without them I could not exist.

CC: You must be very proud of both John and Martin, how they have developed into two of the finest jazz musicians on the scene today. Did you encourage them to take this professional route or did it just evolve?

BP: It sort of happened more than anything else. I didn't push, but music was always around them. John was originally a rock player and one day I challenged him to learn a Django Reinhardt solo. He took the challenge and really got into it, and the rest is history.

CC: What advice would you give to a young jazz guitarist starting out?

BP: I always tell anyone who wants to play guitar to listen to the chords. You have to get the right bass note with the right chord. If you can do this with all the tunes you know you are in the "market place." Before you ever try to play a solo understand where the chords and bass notes go. I find it comforting that I know how to play good rhythm guitar. I have made my living backing up people and continue to work because of this facet of guitar playing. My best advice to any guitar player, in any style, is to learn how to play rhythm and learn how chords work, and everything else will fall in place.

Bucky with grandson John and son.

John Pizzarelli – *(December 1997)*

John was born in 1960 and was introduced to the guitar and banjo at an early age by his father Bucky, and his great uncles Pete and Bobby Domenick. These were the same uncles that inspired his famed father to make music his life. John has fond childhood memories of Benny Goodman dropping by his house, and of growing up in a home where everyone played an instrument. In 1990 he formed the John Pizzarelli trio with Ray Kennedy on piano and his brother Martin on bass. John was inspired to become a jazz vocalist by listening to the vocal styling of the late Nat King Cole. Now John is accumulating as many accolades as a jazz vocalist as he is as a guitarist. He recently completed a three-month run on Broadway in the Johnny Mercer revue Dream and has recorded his seventh album for RCA, *Our Love Is Here To Stay*.

With his virtuosic guitar styling appearing on most of the network talk shows and another album in the works it seemed like a good time to give this very talented musician a call. I finally caught up with him at his home in Manhattan and had a very good conversation about his unique choice of equipment and upcoming projects. The interview took place on December 12, 1997.

Charles Chapman: Tell us a little about what you consider your main guitar.

John Pizzarelli: My main guitar is a seven string made for me by Bob Benedetto. It's a no frills instrument with a laminated top and back. I travel with it constantly and now use it for just about everything—it's a great guitar.

CC: I was not aware that Bob ever used laminates in his guitars.

JP: He usually doesn't. I believe he's only made three. I specifically ordered one that way because I'm not an easy person on an instrument. I do a tremendous amount of traveling, so I wanted something that was light and durable.

CC: What other guitars do you own?

JP: My prize possession is a 1978 Benedetto 7-string that was made for my father. I also have a classical guitar, an Ovation acoustic, Fender Flame and also a Fender Strat.

CC: What is your preference in amplifiers?

JP: My favorite is a late 1950s vintage Fender Tremolux. I also have a Gibson about the same vintage and a early 1980s Mesa Boogie SOB from my rock days. I do not carry an amp when I'm on tour and always request a Fender Twin. I find the Twin a very consistent amp and it gives me a good sound for what I do.

CC: I didn't realize you ever played rock.

JP: Sure, that's how I started. I played in a rock group in high school and also had my own group that played a lot in NY in the 1980s. The group was called Johnny Pick and His Scabs.

CC: How did you migrate to Jazz?

JP: Jazz was always all around me at home, but because of school, friends, etc. I played more on the rock side. One day my father challenged me to learn a Django Reinhardt solo and that was it—I was hooked. I kept coming back to my father asking more and more questions. We started to play together quite a bit at home and decided to do some gigs and we were quite successful. Between 1980 and 1990 most of the gigs were actually with my dad. Finally, Norman Chesky (booking agent and manager) said: "You should really put your own group together and tour to promote yourself." That's when I decided to put the trio together with my brother Martin and Ray Kennedy.

CC: Is the trio where your emphasis is or do you plan to focus your efforts with larger projects like *Our Love Is Here to Stay* album?

JP: I plan on doing bigger projects when they avail themselves, but the trio is my main focus. Martin and I have always gotten along well together, both musically and personally. We grew up with Milt Hinton and Slam Stewart coming to our house and listening to their music. Ray came out of St. Louis, where his father constantly played jazz records for him while he was growing up. He has played with Sonny Stitt, Freddie Hubbard, James Moody and is a big fan of Oscar Peterson. I had met him through my father and he is exactly what I was looking for. He understands what I want to hear and do with the group. The trio is very easy to travel with as it's only three guys, it's an easy haul. We don't need a road crew, wherever we play we are supplied with an acoustic piano, guitar amplifier and sometimes even the upright bass. A road trip is often no more than just me bringing my guitar. Musically and economically it is a perfect fit and I hope we will be together for many years to come. It just makes sense!

CC: How do you prefer to be recorded?

JP: On most of my records I go direct or mic the Tremolux, and always mic the guitar with an RCA 44 microphone.

CC: What are those very unusual strings you have on your guitar?

JP: They are LaBella tape wound strings and they come in a set specifically made for the 7-string guitar. I don't know the exact gauges, but the first two strings are .014 & .018 and the seventh string is 1.00.

CC: What picks do you use?

JP: My favorites are Manny's heavy tortoise shell picks. If I can't get them I use Fender heavy tortoise shell.

CC: Can you tell us about any upcoming projects?

JP: Very shortly I will be recording another big band album with Don Sebesky. It will be on the RCA label and will hopefully be out in the spring of '98.

CC: Here's a question from left field and a great way to end the interview. My editor wants to know how you keep your hair looking so great?

JP: Believe it or not I get that question a lot. I do nothing to it, just wash it and let it dry naturally. My girlfriend tells me I have the best hair in show business.

Photo by Donna Chapman

John Scofield – *(March 1996)*

Photo by Ken Schles

John Scofield grew up in a small town in Connecticut and came to Boston in 1970 to study at Berklee College of Music. He left Berklee to tour with Gerry Mulligan and Chet Baker—playing in their famed Carnegie Hall reunion. He then replaced John Abercrombie in Billy Cobham's band, which led to work with Charles Mingus, Gary Burton and Dave Leibman. In 1982 John began one of the world's highest-profile projects; a several-year, multi-album gig with Miles Davis. His term as the jazz legend's sideman, soloist, and writing partner placed him among the leading guitarists of his generation. With literally dozens of recordings and appearances in worldwide concerts and clinics, he truly has achieved, at a young age, elder statesman stature for Berklee College.

The following interview was conducted on March 22, 1996 at the Lenox Suites Hotel, Chicago, IL. At that time John was performing at the Jazz Showcase with Larry Goldman on keyboards, Dennis Irwin on bass and Idris Muhammad on drums.

Charles Chapman: How old were you when you started to play guitar and what initially drew you to it?

John Scofield: I was eleven, and believe it or not, the Beatles and folk music is what initially drew me into music and guitar.

CC: What made your decision to attend Berklee?

JS: I was initially into the blues and really dug B.B. King, Howlin' Wolf, Muddy Waters and that whole Chicago blues sound. After a few years I decided to take lessons, and was extremely lucky to get an excellent teacher who exposed me to many kinds of music. A fine guitarist, Alan Dean, not only played rock and blues, but was also a superb jazz player. He's the one that turned me on to jazz and I became hooked. Alan was really into Berklee and told me if I was serious about music, Berklee was the place to go.

CC: I can never remember you performing or recording on anything but electric guitar. Recently you have been incorporating acoustic guitar on your recordings and live shows. Is this something new?

JS: The acoustic guitar and I go way back. My mother rented this acoustic guitar for me from the local music store when I was eleven. She didn't want to spend the money on a good instrument. The strings were probably two inches off the neck, and I don't think I could play it today. I had it for about a week, and I couldn't even get a sound from it. So I said, "Mom, I was mistaken. What I really want to do is play the drums." But she said, "No, we rented it for three months, and you're going to stick to it." At the end of three months I could play C, G7 and E, and I was hooked. I migrated away from it for many years, but now I'm firmly entrenched in it again.

CC: What acoustic guitars did you use on the *Groove Elation* album (Blue Note CDP 7243 B 32801 2 4) and do you use the same ones for live performances?

JS: On the *Groove Elation* album I used a 1941 Martin that I bought from Mat Umanoff on Bleaker Street in New York City. I do not know the model, but it has a small body and great tone. I also used that guitar on the album with Pat Metheny. It's a real collectors item, and too fragile to take on the road or use live. On live performances I use a Guild with a Fishman setup for amplification. I also bought a beautiful flamenco guitar made by a company in Berkley, California called Montaldo. I plan on using this on my next record. On live performances I also use a Sadowsky nylon string.

CC: What are you thoughts about developing improvisational skills?

JS: Improvising is getting your musical thoughts out on your instrument. A lot of guitarists practice things that aren't actually their musical thoughts, and are purely physical exercises, and that has no meaning to me at all as far as creating music is concerned. Merely how fast someone can play—that's not important at all. The thing is pulling off the musical effects you want when you are improvising. Don't be afraid to play old licks when the time is right. Everybody repeats themselves to a degree. Improvising is using your musical vocabulary to fit the moment and make it work. Sometimes you actually improvise, you actually pull some stuff out of the hat. Mainly it's being able to use what you already know.

CC: Was there anyone specific that shaped your improvisational style?

JS: There were really a lot of great musicians that I listened to over the years that molded my style. Miles, and definitely Steve Swallow come to mind. Steve specifically made an impact and helped me develop into a mature musician. He showed me how to make a statement and get some sort of architecture to a piece of music, instead of just going nuts every time. The goal of creative music is to play what you hear, it's not just moving your fingers around.

CC: You often use New Orleans based players. Do you feel they have a different "vibe" than players from other areas?

JS: I'm a big fan of New Orleans music. There is a particular type of groove that lives in the R&B and Latin rhythms they play. This whole "beat thing" exists that you can't put your finger on, but you can feel it. I've used Idris Muhammad on many of my projects and he's really from the scene. He grew up playing with the Neville Brothers and all that true New Orleans "Mardi Gras Indian" type groove. I also enjoy, and intend on working with, Johnny Vidacovich and Ricky Sebastian in the near future.

CC: For a number of years now you've been fronting groups as opposed to being a sideman. Could you comment on that?

JS: When it's my group it's generally my tunes we play; I call the shots, and have all the headaches. That's where it ends because on the bandstand we're musical equals. That's the way it should be. I have played in bands where I am a lot stronger than the rhythm section. It doesn't feel good to me. I like to have that strength around me. I'm addicted to it. So, it may be the John Scofield Group and the album

has a big picture of me, but the honest-to-God truth is that once you count off the tune and everybody is playing, we are all in there together.

CC: Do you have any new albums in the works?

JS: Yes, I'm in the process of writing the music for a new album right now, and plan on going in the studio in a few weeks. I'll be playing primarily acoustic guitar and the album will have a Latin/Brazilian sort of feel. I will use some electric, but it will mainly be acoustic guitar with the emphasis being on nylon string. I'm going to score it for six horns and rhythm section. I guess I'll have to dig out some of my old Berklee arranging books.

CC: Who else is on the album with you?

JS: Steve Swallow on bass, Bill Stewart on drums and another drummer from Brazil named Daduca Dafonsecka. Wayne Shorter will also be playing on a few tunes.

CC: What advice could you give students heading for a career in music?

JS: Don't get too cynical. Trying to cope with the strange business side of music and make a living can drive anybody crazy. I've seen myself and everybody else go through changes about career and creativity, but what really counts in the end is the music. I'm not saying that from a purist attitude, and I realize as well as the next person that you have to pay your rent, but trying to make great music makes the difference. The commitment to craft, and playing really well is what it's all about. Musicians often get lost in the day to day drudgeries and tend to get very cynical. Making the best music you can is the only way to ultimately achieve success, recognition, and truly have fun.

John with his first guitar.

Johnny Smith – *(September 1996)*

At the '96 Nashville NAMM Show Johnny Smith, the legendary jazz guitarist, made an unprecedented appearance to preside over an international guitar competition. His reclusive behavior has made Smith sightings as rare as extraterrestrial ones. To many his signature Gibson Guitar—which has been the epitome of the jazz guitar sound for over thirty years—is their only connection to this guitar great. It's no wonder the masses are unfamiliar with Johnny Smith, as he semi-retired from the rigors of a performance career in the 1960s and moved to Colorado. There he owned and managed his own music store/studio, only surfacing occasionally to conduct jazz seminars and a few rare appearances with the late Bing Crosby.

Johnny Smith was born in Birmingham, Alabama on June 25, 1922. His initial interest in music came from his father who played 5-string banjo. His major influences were Django Reinhardt and Andrés Segovia— as is very evident in his incredibly precise chord voicings and at times machine gun-like 16th note solo phrasing. He gained his first musical experience playing in a country group called the Fenton Brothers in 1939. In 1940 he moved to Boston to perform in the burgeoning jazz scene and stayed there until he was drafted in the air force. After his discharge in 1947, the NBC network in New York City hired him as their staff guitarist. During the next seven years he honed his craft playing in multitudes of venues from small settings to full orchestras. He also achieved legendary stature during this time for his ability to sight-read virtually anything, and to perform burning improvisational solos over any type of chord progressions (still a rare commodity in 1996).

In the 1950s he achieved critical acclaim for his newly formed quintet with tenor saxophonist Stan Getz. The quintet went on to have the number one jazz album of 1952, *Moonlight in Vermont. Moonlight in Vermont* was the signature tune of the album of the same name which earned him the title "King of Cool Jazz Guitar." During this era, Johnny won every jazz award possible: Downbeat Best Jazz Guitarist, Best Jazz Record, Jazz Critic's Award, Metronome Poll, etc. To quote the great jazz guitarist Pat Martino: "Johnny Smith is the epitome of precision and getting out what you want to say without laboring over impediments. When I listen and view Smith's mastery of the guitar I seriously want to become another Johnny Smith."

Seeing Johnny in action again piqued my interest, and in September 1996 I gave him a call to chat and get some insight into this great guitar icon.

Charles Chapman: What guitarists in the last few years have you taken an interest in?

Johnny Smith: There are many outstanding guitarists performing now, but a few that immediately comes to mind are Jack Wilkins, Howard Alden and Mark Whitfield.

CC: How many albums have you recorded?

JS: I never really sat down and counted them, but I believe around thirty.

CC: What was your favorite album?

JS: I don't like any of them! This is not meant as an excuse in any way, but back in the days when I was recording we had to record extremely fast with very little time for rehearsal or retakes. Time was money, and it was a union rule that you had to record four sides in three hours. A lot of times you would just have to play very conservatively and make as few blatant mistakes as possible.

CC: Did you use any special recording techniques to capture your sound in the studio?

JS: That's a sore subject with me because I always had to fight like hell with the engineers. They always wanted me to separate the players, putting the piano in one corner, the bass in another corner, and the drums somewhere else. When you're playing jazz you have to interact and communicate, and you can't do that properly if you can't hear the instruments correctly or can't look the players in the eye. Another aspect that always aggravated me was when the sound wasn't right on stage and people would tell me not to worry about it because it was fine out in the audience. If it doesn't sound good where you're playing, you just can't perform creative music to the best of your ability.

CC: How did you develop your technique?

JS: I always had great admiration for other instrumentalists such as the piano, violin and other orchestral instruments. They had proven standards and methodology for learning, and I tried to adapt their techniques to the guitar. I would often practice from violin, clarinet or flute books.

CC: When did Gibson start making your signature guitar?

JS: When I decided to settle down in Colorado and open a music store is when I initially endorsed Gibson. They had been after me for a number of years to work with them, but I just didn't have the time. In the early 1960s I wanted to settle down and start my own business, and the collaboration with Gibson gave me the financial means to do this.

CC: How much input did you have on the design and construction of the guitar?

JS: I had complete control and designed the entire guitar myself. The only aspect Gibson had was some of the cosmetic touches which I couldn't care less about. I designed how the guitar would be braced, how the top would be carved, the dimensions, binding— everything.

CC: I was not aware you were schooled in guitar construction. Where did you acquire this knowledge?

JS: During the years I lived in New York I spent a lot of time in the workshop of my dear friend, John D'Angelico. He and his young apprentice, Jimmy D'Aquisto, taught me how a guitar should be made. John made the finest guitars I ever played, and when I decided to endorse and play a Gibson I really felt embarrassed. I went to John and explained how I felt; and he replied that he could only build so many guitars, so if I could help a company put out a good-quality instrument I would be doing everyone a favor. He was truly a gentleman.

CC: How many D'Angelico guitars have you owned?

JS: I've played three and they were all the same superb quality. The first one was destroyed in a fire when my house burned down on Long Island. John Collins, the guitarist for Nat King Cole, let me use his D'Angelico while John D. built another one for me. John D'Angelico finished my new guitar in 1955 and I used it until I entered my agreement with Gibson.

CC: Do you still own that guitar?

JS: No, I relinquished it a few years after I went with Gibson, to Hank Risan who is now a guitar collector.

CC: What amplifiers have you owned in the past?

JS: Amplifiers were another major problem in performing. With the acoustic-body guitar it was a constant fight to come up with an amplifier that would sound like an extension of the guitar. I could not find one commercially available that I liked. Everett Hull founder of the Ampeg company finally built one for me that I could live with. Gibson also designed and built one from my specifications that I used for a number of years. The only other amplifier I ever liked was a transistor model, made by a small company in Denver called Emrad. It was made to sound like my Gibson and it worked well, in fact, I still own it. Most amp companies have too much on the high and low end and not enough mid-range. To amplify acoustic guitar it's the mid range that's important. On all my amps if I turned the bass control to 10 it would have less bass than most Fenders when the bass control is on 0.

CC: Could you give us a run down on your strings and picks?

JS: My favorite strings are not made any more. They were Black Diamond #100 series burnished strings. They were not round or flat wound, but something in between. I used a stock set that was .012 to .052 but changed the 6th string to a .056 to accommodate my tuning. I always tuned my low E to D to have a wider range and expand my chord range. I only use heavy picks.

CC: For years a story has circulated that in the prime of your career you severed the end off the ring finger of your left hand, had it re-attached, and continued on with your playing. Is there any truth to this story?

JS: The end of my finger was ripped off in an accident in 1963, but they were not able to re-attach it. Skin was taken from the palm of my hand and the end of my finger was rebuilt. It hung me up for about a year, but I was able to play again. The only problem was that the end of my finger was a quarter of an inch shorter and I had to re-adjust my playing.

CC: I remember vividly a TV special you were on with Bing Crosby. In that special you were playing great fills, solos and comping. Were those parts written or were sketch arrangements used?

JS: When you played with Bing there was no music. You were expected to know all his tunes and arrangements from his records. He would call the tunes and you were on your own.

CC: Is there any gig or period of time in your career that stands out from the rest?

JS: Yes, my years in New York with NBC. I feel very fortunate that I was in the business in what I consider the apex of music. For example in the late '40s and '50s the studios all used live music. Toscanini was at NBC when I was there, and all the three networks used live music. There were over 100 musicians employed full time to play for the shows. Live music was everywhere right down to the commercials not only on TV, but radio as well. I feel bad for many musicians today who have great difficulty finding outlets to perform and use there talents.

CC: Do you have any advice for musicians starting out?

JS: You have to love it enough to survive the hardships of attaining your goal. To attain your goal, whatever that may be—has to be your reward.

Photo by Donna Chapman

Johnny Smith at the Smithsonian Institute with guitar collector Scott Chinery.

Photo by Donna Chapman

Mike Stern – (November 1999)

Mike was born on January 10, 1953 and began playing guitar at age 12 with his main influences being Jimi Hendrix, Eric Clapton and B.B. King. When he was eighteen he entered Berklee College and became enamored by the music of Bill Evans, Sonny Rollins, Wes Montgomery, Jim Hall and started to develop his unique jazz style often referred to as "bop and roll."

In 1975 he joined Blood Sweat & Tears and continued on with the Brecker Brothers, David Sanborn, Jaco Pastorius and Miles Davis.

Mike's own music has been his main focus for many years and has released nine albums under his own name on the Atlantic label. His most recent is *Play*, featuring Berklee alumni guitarists Bill Frisell and John Scofield. Mike has returned to Berklee numerous times to preside over clinics and concerts, his most recent visit was during the "1999 Berklee Summer Guitar Sessions." Mike leads a grueling tour schedule performing to ecstatic audiences all over the globe. I was able to catch up with him in Copenhagen, Denmark while he was on a Scandinavian Tour.

Charles Chapman: Since you left college in 1975 to start your career as a performing musician what changes are the most apparent in the industry?

Mike Stern: Jazz guitar in general seems to be more excepting and open than it used to be. Any guitarist growing up in the '60s and early '70s could not ignore Jimi Hendrix, B.B. King, Eric Clapton with the Creme or Jeff Beck, Albert King, etc. Those guys became part of guitarist's style and vocabulary, but for a while it was not accepted in the jazz world, but now jazz is much more open. From my generation on there seems to be more acceptance in jazz of different styles that came from rock or funk and I think it's great. It's an amazing time to be a guitarist, as guitar is everywhere—it is in pop, jazz, classical and everything in between.

CC: Were there any particular teachers that stand out in your mind from your Berklee years?

MS: My first guitar teacher at Berklee was Larry Senibaldi who was great. He was so clear, supportive and also a wonderful player. I studied briefly with Pat Metheny who introduced me to Mick Goodrick. Mick definitely had a major influence on my playing and style. He's an amazing innovator who's had a large impact on the evolution of modern day jazz guitar.

CC: Charlie Banacos seems to be your mentor, both past and present. How did you meet him and how has he changed the way you perceive music and play guitar?

CC: I originally heard about Charlie when I was in Boston and he's an amazing jazz teacher. He's a piano player, but accepts all musicians no matter what instrument they play. He has this incredible way of organizing and being able to teach. He inspires you to play and feel that you really can become a great musician. I took lessons with him when I lived in Boston and now study with him through a correspondence course he offers. He has about a three year waiting list, but it is well worth it. Jerry Bergonzi is another guy in the Boston area who's an amazing teacher and also one of the greatest tenor players alive.

CC: Your sound is very distinctive. What sound processing do you use and how did you arrive at it?

MS: I was always looking for a fat kind of sound in terms of legato, sort of horn like. So sound processing seems to help that. I use a Yamaha SPX 90 which is kind of old, but I really like it. By today's standards my equipment setup is very minimal. I use the SPX 90 with two amps in stereo and that is my basic sound, whether I am in the studio or live. It doesn't matter how much or little equipment you use, the idea is to get a sound you are comfortable with so you can get to the heart of the music. Anything that can help get your emotions into your music is what you should strive for.

CC: Do you feel that developing that emotional intensity is one of your main ingredients to your success and longevity as a jazz musician?

MS: It might be part of it, but the key is not to force your sound. Let it come naturally and develop as you progress as a musician. Transcribing is great, but don't just do one style or one particular musician. Finding your own voice is generally a combination of different things you have heard other players do. You should transcribe Jim Hall one day and Eric Clapton the next. Find out what you like about their playing and try to incorporate it into your style. Developing this type of vocabulary is the tradition of being a jazz musician.

CC: What do you have in the works for the millennium?

MS: I just released a CD that I am very excited about titled: *Play* on the Atlantic label. It features two of my best friends and favorite guitarists, John Scofield and Bill Frisell. Also Dennis Chambers, Bob Malick, Lincoln Goines and Ben Perowski are a part of this project. Hopefully, in the near future I will be signing a multi-CD contract with Atlantic Records and my touring schedule is looking very active for the millennium. Anyone who is interested can check my website at: wwwmikestern.org for my gigs, concerts, recordings and a lot of other interesting stuff.

CC: You have an extremely active worldwide touring schedule. How do you cope with that type of life?

MS: Sometimes it drives me crazy, but if you want to promote your music you have to take it to the people—and touring is the name of the game. My wife Leni goes on the road a lot for her gigs, so we try to coordinate it so we are both away at the same time. Sometimes she will travel with me. It's all a balancing act.

CC: Any general advice for guitarists embarking on a career in music?

MS: Music is definitely a language so make sure you learn the vocabulary and keep playing and listening. Just remember that music is the mother tongue of emotion and just play from the heart.

Martin Taylor – (January 2001)

Martin Taylor was born on October 20, 1956 Harlow, Essex, United Kingdom. At age four his father, jazz bassist Buck Taylor, gave him a small acoustic guitar. By age eleven he had his first electric, a Guild Starfire, and was listening intently to the recordings of Barney Kessel, Kenny Burrel and Wes Montgomery. He was also was fascinated by the piano styling of Bill Evans and Art Tatum which was to mold his solo career many years later.

Martin garnered International recognition in the late 1970s through his collaborations with the French violin legend Stephane Grappelli. This was the beginning of an eleven-year collaboration and over 20 albums including recordings with Michel Legrand, Peggy Lee, Yehudi Menuhin, Nelson Riddle and several film soundtracks including the Louis Malle movie *Milou En Mai* and the Steve Martin/Michael Caine film *Dirty Rotten Scoundrels*. Martin is also a jazz guitar icon in his own right having released approximately a dozen albums under his own name with his most recent being *Kiss and Tell* on the Sony label. He has also recently released an autobiography by the same name.

Martin has collaborated with many musicians outside the jazz world including Yes guitarist Steve Howe and classical guitarist Carlos Bonell. He is also featured on the Prefab Sprout album *Andromeda Heights* and plays alongside Eric Clapton, Peter Frampton and Albert Lee on Bill Wyman's Rhythm Kings albums. In 1998 Martin appeared in the historic Blue Guitar Concert at Wolf Trap Center for the Performing Arts in Vienna, VA with legendary guitarists such as George Benson, Kenny Burrel, Larry Coryell and John Pizzarelli. *The Washington Post* made special note of Martin's performance by commenting in their Performing Arts Column: "No matter how complex or daring, Taylor's interpretation never short change the melodies; indeed, his remarkable fluid touch imbues a seamless beauty. Taylor is something to behold."

Martin Taylor is truly a guitarist who does it all!

On December 1, 2000 Martin took time out of his very busy schedule to speak with Charles about his music, new book, equipment and upcoming touring schedule.

Charles Chapman: How did you first meet Stephane Grappelli?

Martin Taylor: I met Stephane through a friend, Ike Isaacs. Ike was a very fine jazz guitarist and had worked with Stephane and made the introductions. Stephane came to hear me play and everything just fell into place. I worked with him for many years performing and recording in all types of venues. Most of the major tours were actually in the United States. He was a great man and I miss him dearly.

CC: I couldn't help but notice your Yamaha guitar has been autographed by Chet Atkins. What's that all about?

MT: (Laughs) I am often asked to perform at the Chet Atkins convention, a yearly Nashville event. One particular year we were sitting backstage and fans kept coming up to Chet asking him to sign their guitars. I was sitting there having a drink, just watching and said: "Hey Chet, how about signing mine." It's like getting a tattoo, it seemed like the thing to do at the time.

CC: Tell us a little about your Vanden Guitar.

MT: Mike Vanden is a very skilled guitar maker in Scotland. We have now designed two guitars together, an archtop and a flat-top. The archtop is called "The Martin Taylor Artistry" and the flat-top is the "The Martin Taylor Gypsy." The idea is not for Mike to actually make the guitars, but we have formed a guitar design company and are in the process of going into production to have them manufactured.

CC: I'm told you have quite a collection of instruments. Are you a collector?

MT: I'm not really a collector, I just love guitars. Actually, I have let many wonderful instruments slip through my fingers. At one time I owned a Johnny Smith as well as a 1935 Maccaferri that were just tremendous guitars. I still own quite a few instruments, but there's really no collection.

CC: What are some of your instruments?

MT: In 1988 Bob Benedetto made me a beautiful Cremona model which was featured on the album cover of my solo project *Portraits*. I have a 1929 Martin 00045, Gibson Eddie Lang L4 model, 1935 Epiphone Deluxe, a few mandolins, and quite a few various other instruments.

CC: I've always been curious about the arrangement of *Blue Bossa* that you and Steve Howe worked on using the twenty-two different "Blue Guitars" from the Chinery Collection. Tell us about that experiment.

MT: Guitar collector Scott Chinery, decided to record a project featuring guitars from his collection, and hired Steve Howe and myself. As it turned out Steve turned into more of an advisor and only played on two or three tunes. Scott wanted a song that would feature all the guitars from his "Blue Guitar Collection." The Blue Guitars were conceived by Scott to honor famed luthier Jimmy D'Aquisto. D'Aquisto's favorite color was blue, as was one of the last guitars he built before he died. Scott consigned twenty-two of the finest archtop builders to make blue guitars for this historic collection. I immediately thought of the tune *Blue Bossa* because it was short and had a nice harmonic groove to it. To my amazement, neither Scott or Steve had ever heard of it, but told me to run with it and do what I wanted. I played a different Blue Guitar for the melody and each solo chorus. I thought it only fitting to use the D'Aquisto on all the rhythm tracks as if Jimmy was listening to each of the guitars built in his honor. It was a great experience.

CC: Were there any particular guitar or guitars that stood out?

MT: All the guitars were incredible in construction, sound and playability, but four really "spoke to me." The D'Aquisto of course, Bob Benedetto's "La Cremona Azzurra," Linda Manzer's "Blue Absynthe" and John Montelone's "Rocket Convertible." These four guitars particularly fascinated me in all aspects.

CC: I heard you perform *Mona Lisa* twice. Once at the Smithsonian Institution and again at Wolf Trap. The combination of that arrangement and the Benedetto La Cremona Azzurra was just breathtaking. Why did you pick that arrangement and that particular guitar to perform it on?

MT: I picked that tune because it was my Dad's favorite and because I really enjoy performing it (also featured on current album *Kiss and Tell*). I decided to use Bob's guitar because it is a wonderful instrument and just seemed right for the venue and tune.

CC: Your solo guitar concerts are just astounding, how and why did you head in that direction?

MT: I was always fascinated with the guitar as a complete instrument. When I was younger I would listen to piano players and admire the way they could accompany themselves and be self-contained. When I was performing with Stephane he liked to feature me on a solo piece every night and I always received a great response from the audience. Around 1986 I was asked to perform a solo concert and it was the first time I ever played a complete concert all alone and it went very well. It was not something I set out to do, but more of an evolution of what the people wanted to hear from me. Now it's the most comfortable genre I perform in.

CC: Are there any particular warm-up exercises you do on a daily basis?

MT: No, I just play. That's really the truth! I just pick up the guitar and try to figure things out. I've never had a teacher and am completely self taught. Since I was four years old that's how I've done it.

CC: So you don't have a practice regime that you adhere to?

MT: No, not at all. Generally I work on what I need to work on for the particular project, whether it's a recording or concert series. That usually means figuring out what tunes I want to play and how I want to play them. Again, I'm self-taught and try to play what I hear; there's no real methodology to it. When I'm not on the road, which is rare, I only pick up the guitar when I feel like it. Some days I will only play for five minutes and occasionally will go for days without even touching it.

CC: After a respite away from your instrument does it take you long to get your groove back?

MT: No, sometimes I even play better when I pick the guitar up again. You must remember that I've had a guitar in my hands since I was four years old and it is very natural thing for me to do.

CC: Do you read music and what is your approach to improvisation?

MT: I only read minimally. If you give me a piece of music I can figure it out, but reading is not my strong point. As far as improvisation goes, I have always had music around and when I first started playing I always jammed with people who were better than me. I would hear what they did and try to emulate it. I've always done a lot of listening and my main objective is to just get the ear/hand relationship as one.

CC: Please give us the rundown on your equipment.

MT: I am now using the Vanden flat-top and archtop guitars with AER amplification from Germany. Round-wound Elixir strings gauges, .012 to .052, with Jim Dunlop "Gator Grip" picks. I am awfully hard on strings. In fact, I can barely get one gig out of most brands. The Elixirs are the only strings I've ever used that I could actually get five or six gigs from, which means for most players they could probably get weeks or even months out of a set.

CC: Please tell us a little about what your recent endeavors as well as any upcoming events or projects that you are involved in.

MT: I'm just finishing up a tour. I did two large solo concerts in Japan— one in Tokyo and the other in Nagoya. I was in New Zealand performing at the World Guitar Series in Auckland and Wellington. Recently, I was invited to the Manchester Craftsman Guild in Pittsburgh, PA performing five concerts with a band. David Newton on piano, Gene Caldalato on drums, Dwayne Dolphin on bass, Randy Breaker on flugel and trumpet, and Kim Walters on sax. It was recorded for a PBS special which should be aired in the US sometime in 2001. I will be back in the States to record my second Sony album after the first of the year. My web page has been redesigned and upgraded which I am very proud of (www.martintaylor.com). I was approached by a large publishing house to write an autobiography and it was just released. It's entitled: *Kiss and Tell -The Autobiography of a Traveling Musician*. In fact, as we speak I am now on a book-signing tour. The album of the same name was released in the UK a year ago and recently in the States. Next week I am going to try to get a few days rest at my home in Scotland, then I have a TV appearance in London followed by 5 days in Thailand. I've been asked to play a solo concert for the King of Thailand. It's his 73rd birthday and he's a big jazz fan, he plays clarinet and alto sax. The King also composes and I will perform a few of his compositions during the Bangkok concert. Next year I will be spending a lot more time in the States than I have in the past and hopefully a lot of exciting things are starting to happen.

CC: What advice would you give someone who wanted to make music a career?

MT: From the moment I started to play guitar it was all I ever wanted to do. I never thought of it as a career, it's just something I had to do. Play music for the sake of making music. If you can make a living from it, then it's a plus. If you can make a career out of it, then it's even a bigger bonus. If you can make a lot of money from it, then it's truly a miracle.

Photo by Donna Chapman

Martin and Charles at the Smithsonian Institute with Bob Benedetto's blue guitar.

Andy Timmons — (March 1995)

Andy Timmons has long been recognized as a guitar virtuoso within the music community. His ability to play with conviction in almost any style has brought him to the forefront of today's players.

A veteran of the international rock band circuit, Andy was recruited by EPIC recording group, Danger Danger in 1989. In 1990 Danger Danger embarked on numerous world tours with bands such as Kiss, Warrant, Alice Cooper and Extreme. The band enjoyed the accolades of two Top 10 videos on MTV and extensive media coverage.

Andy is presently an endorsee and clinician for Ibanez, Hughes & Kettner and Mesa Boogie. His debut CD *Ear X-tacy* is an instrumental masterpiece and as stated by *Guitar World Magazine*, is a fine showcase of chops and musical intelligence.

Andy is also an active clinician for schools and workshops throughout the country, and is currently living in Austin, TX where this interview took place.

Charles Chapman: Recently you were a clinician for Guitar Week '94 at Berklee College in Boston. Did you find the guitar students there any different from students in other schools you visit?

Andy Timmons: The only aspect I found different were the numbers. I was amazed at the incredible number of guitar students at Berklee. My brief visit was very enjoyable, and I found the students extremely energetic and eager to learn. It was a great atmosphere that I'd like to be around more often. That raw desire to learn is incredible and I can still remember that feeling from when I attended the University of Miami—and I often miss it.

CC: Are you a schooled guitarist or did you learn by your own devices?

AT: I initially taught myself and learned totally by ear. By eighth grade I was in a band and performing constantly. As I became more serious I studied classical guitar for a few years and also had a jazz teacher. I was lucky to have had wonderful teachers who were not only knowledgeable, but were caring and truly interested in me.

CC: Is the University of Miami where you studied classical guitar?

AT: No, I studied it privately when I was in my teens and also was a classical guitar major at the University of Evansville, Indiana my home town. I later attended the University of Miami where I studied jazz guitar.

CC: Who were some of your early influences?

AT: Ace Frehley from Kiss, Rush, Foghat and definitely Ted Nugent. Then as I progressed my influences changed constantly.

CC: On your album *Ear X-tacy* you played a tune called *No More Good-Byes* and it seemed to have a great deal of influence derived from Pat Metheny.

AT: You're right. In fact, I consider that tune my tribute to Pat. He's a great guitarist and was, and still is a major influence for me.

CC: I can definitely hear the classical and jazz influence in your playing—would you recommend that students study classical and jazz?

AT: I know it was a great help to me, but as I think back I can't say it was classical or jazz lessons that helped me as much as great teachers. I think the teacher is what is really important, more than the style. If you have a knowledgeable teacher who cares about you, the style is not that important.

CC: You played some great jazz lines on the tune *It's Getting Better* and the 8va lines on *There Are No Words* were equally as good. I'm curious as to why you cut both these sections short. Were you trying to stay away from a jazz sound?

AT: Definitely not, it was just the way I heard it and I really liked the way those two takes came out.

CC: One of the aspects of your playing that has duly impressed me is your command of the instrument. Do you practice technique exercises or is that something that has developed with your playing.

AT: I do have exercises for developing technique, but I feel my command of the instrument comes mainly from playing. From an early age I was performing in bands and I feel that developed my technique better than anything else.

CC: Do you still compose for the sake of writing or is it usually project oriented?

AT: Both, I try to write and then incorporate it into projects at a later date, but many times I have a project in mind and my writing is geared in that direction.

CC: Are there any projects you have underway that you could discuss?

AT: Yes, at the moment I have three projects in the works. The first is a CD of a blues band called the *Pawn Kings*, I formed it just to have fun and play this small club on Wednesday nights. The group caught on and we decided to put out a CD. The second is a follow up to *Ear X-tacy* and I'm basically using the same people. The third is a vocal album doing everything from blues to Hendrix and even a little Elvis Costello and Beatles.

CC: What do you consider your main axe?

AT: I own a number of guitars, but my main axe is a Ibanez custom 570. It has one humbucker and two single coil DIMarzio pickups. I've been playing it for a long time and it does just about everything I want it to do.

CC: What is your live rig like?

AT: I actually have a few different setups. For small clubs I use a 35 watt Mesa/Boogie Maverick slaved to a Rocktron Intellifex that feeds two Peavy Bandit amps. For larger venues the rig gets a lot more complicated, but the basic setup is an ADA MP1 pre amp going through Mesa and Marshall cabs.

CC: What advice would you give students about to embark on a career in music?

AT: Play the music you love and give it all you've got. When you do that you can't go wrong.

Jack Wilkins — (April 2000)

Jack Wilkins was born in Brooklyn, NY and has now been a part of the New York jazz scene for more than four decades. His flawless technique and imaginative chordal approach have inspired collaborations with Chet Baker, Sarah Vaughan, Bob Brookmeyer, Buddy Rich, Eddie Gomez, Brecker Brothers, Ray Charles, Tony Bennett, Dizzy Gillespie, Benny Goodman, Stan Getz and countless others. Jack currently lives in Manhattan, NY and teaches at The New School and Manhattan School of Music. He conducts seminars and clinics throughout the US.

In recent years Jack has been extremely active, performing in many international festivals including the Sydney Jazz Festival, the Stockholm Jazz Festival, the Switzerland Jazz Festival, the Berlin Jazz Festival, and virtually every major festival in the US.

He is also a prolific writer and arranger having written more than 60 original compositions and was the primary arranger for the project *The Mingus Epitaph, 5 Guitars Play Mingus* with bassist Eddie Gomez.

In 1977 Nat Hentoff wrote the following about Jack after hearing him in Buddy Rich's club in Manhat-

tan: "His sound was glowing; his ideas were freshly, subtly imaginative; and he communicated an openness of spirit, and enveloping warmth..." Twenty-three years later, things have not changed!

I caught up to Jack for a one-to-one in Boston on March 10, 2000 and also had a very pleasant conversation with him at his home on March 12th. The following are a few of his thoughts and opinions on guitar and music in general.

Charles Chapman: Was music a part of your family life during your formative years?

JW: Yes, my mother sang great and also played a little piano. My stepfather played trombone and saxophone and was in a big band. We always had music playing in our house; like Frank Sinatra, Tony Bennett, Billie Holiday. I originally started on guitar and then I got into vibes very seriously for three or four years. In fact, I had a jazz group when I was in my teens called The Jazz Partners where I played vibes and Barry Manilow was the piano player.

CC: When did you get serious about playing guitar?

JW: When I was about eighteen, but I was always serious about music.

CC: Did you formally study music?

JW: I almost went to Berklee, but the tuition was a little high for me to handle, so I studied privately and worked on many facets of music besides performing. I studied arranging, theory, harmony and was extremely serious about learning everything I could about music.

CC: Who or what made your decision to become a jazz guitarist?

JW: Johnny Smith was the one who made me want to play music. It was his sound, not that he was a guitar player. I never really thought of it as jazz, just great emotional music. I don't feel that I am a guitar player. I'm a musician that plays music on the guitar. I happen to migrate to guitar and I love the sound, but if I played the trumpet, trombone, piano, or whatever, I would play the same. The instrument is just the vehicle to get out what I hear and have in my head. It's all relative—time, rhythm, feel—it's universal. The concept of a jazz guitar is preposterous—it's just music and you get it out with whatever means you have available.

CC: What's the model, and if possible the specs, of that beautiful Benedetto guitar I always hear you playing?

JW: My first Benedetto guitar was made in 1988, it is a 17", traditional sunburst with one Benedetto B-6 humbucker. The neck width is 1¾" with X-bracing. Bob made a second guitar for me a decade later— a Fratello Custom in 1998. It also is a 17" traditional sunburst, but has a neck width of 1¹¹⁄₁₆" with parallel bracing, two pickups, master volume, master tone (push/pull) and toggle switch with two pickups.

CC: What is the joke I always hear about you playing the "Towel Farlow" model Benedetto?

JW: (Laughs) You should probably ask Bob Benedetto about that. He tells the story better than me.

Bob Benedetto: My guitars usually don't feedback, but occasionally, however, feedback rears its ugly head and the fun begins.

One such case is the custom Fratello model I made for Jack Wilkins (back in 1988), a very pretty 17" sunburst that played and sounded great from day one. The original floating pickup was replaced with my built-in B-6 model—better suited for Jack. I can't imagine any serious guitar enthusiast not knowing what a virtuoso Jack Wilkins is, so imagine his frustration when in most playing situations he had to deal with feedback. For reasons unknown to me, his guitar was more prone to it than most others.

Having exhausted all avenues known to me to correct the problem, I finally "threw in the towel"—literally! I stuffed the body with an old terry cloth towel, crude, perhaps even unprofessional and ungodlike, but it worked!! It's not an original idea either, but is a quick, easy fix to a rather complex problem.

Now Jack plays and smiles, and fears not the nightmare of feedback. He's called me three separate times since I "fixed" his guitar to say that he's never been happier and affectionately refers to it as the "Towel" Farlow model!"

Resuming with Jack Wilkins:

CC: What other guitars do you own?

JW: I also have a 1961 Fender Telecaster that I love and use quite a bit, as well as a nylon string DeCarlo.

CC: What amps, strings, picks or other gear are in your arsenal?

JW: I have seven or eight different amps. I have a few Polytones and a few old Fenders that I really love. I use LaBella flat wound strings—usually the set that starts with .013.

CC: Does your live setup differ from your studio rig?

JW: Not really, I want the sound to be that same as when I play live. I do like to use reverb, but that's about it.

CC: For many years you have conducted clinics for colleges and schools all over the country. Have you noticed any major changes in music students?

JW: Definitely! Students in general seem to be overwhelmed with information and seem to have trouble processing it. Many just seem to be in sensory overload. Information in itself is nothing if you do not know how to put it in practical use.

CC: Are there any general practice procedures you would recommend for the budding jazz guitarist to include in their daily routine?

JW: Play music that you do not normally play, like Mozart or possibly Beethoven string quartets. Learning literature that you normally would not play will give you a new perspective and insight.

CC: If you had to name one weakness in the young jazz guitarists you encounter, what would that be?

JW: Interaction! They can play all kinds of stuff, but it is very inorganic. It's the chemistry between two musicians that is what makes it happen and too many young musicians just don't get it. They don't play enough with people and when they do it is often with sequenced material. I have nothing against sequencers, sound processing etc., but to become a creative musician one must learn to interact with their fellow musicians, and all too often, it just isn't happening.

CC: I have heard you and Jimmy Bruno perform on numerous occasions and the two of you have a very unique chemistry. Are there any plans in the works for future concerts or recordings?

JW: Yes, this June, Jimmy and I have a gig on the QE II and when we get to England we are going to do an album for the String Jazz Label.

CC: Can you share with us any upcoming projects you have in the works?

JW: I recently released an album for String Jazz titled *Bluesin*. I recorded a project with Gene Bertoncini last year that should soon be release on the Chiaroscuro Label and of course the project in June with Jimmy.

CC: Any concerts or gigs?

JW: Glad you asked! I am performing in concert on April 15th with the Benedetto Players at the Melville Marriott on Long Island, NY that should be great! I will be playing with two other great guitarists, Frank Vignola and Howard Alden. I also have a great solo guitar gig every Sunday on 53rd and 2nd in Manhattan, it is at a very nice little place called Askew. I can play whatever I want and often have friends sit in, the audience is very receptive. I've had the gig for about a month and, hopefully, will be there for quite a while.

CC: You have mentioned that you felt the greatest era of all times could be approaching for musicians. What did you mean by that?

JW: I mean that given the internet and the great volume of material available—if musicians, and especially students, can learn to process what they have available to them, unbelievable things could happen. They have to be able to put into practical use what they learn. It seems to me that many students are overwhelmed with information, but if they can learn to listen, interact and keep the love of the art— great things will be in store for the millennium.

Andy Summers and Jack in concert.

Photo by Donna Chapman

From Van Eps to Vai and Beyond — *(November 1997)*

With Quotes from George Van Eps, Bucky Pizzarelli, Howard Alden,
Bob Benedetto, Bill Conklin, Fred Fried and Steve Vai.

The 7-string guitar is making a resurgence and once again, manufacturers and private luthiers are tooling up to make these guitars available to the masses. Because the interest in this instrument is escalating to a new high, in the rock and jazz circles, I decided to delve into its very eclectic history starting with the father of the 7-string guitar—George Van Eps.

According to most, George Van Eps is the first archtop guitarist to utilize the extra low A string. In fact, even today most of the 7-string jazz artists consider George their linchpin to the instrument. George notes, "The reason for my wanting the additional low A string was based on my love of deep basslines, and because I approached the guitar as a complete instrument in itself, like a mini-orchestra."

In the 1940s, the Epiphone company built a custom 7-string guitar to George's specifications. It was a Masterbuilt-era Epiphone Deluxe with a custom 7-string neck. He started playing a Gretsch in 1968 when he landed a Baldwin endorsement (Baldwin purchased Gretsch in 1966). Gretsch produced the Van Eps single-cutaway model from 1968 until 1972 (in '72, consumers could get the model 7580 in

George Van Eps

Photo by Dr. Frank Forte

sunburst and 7581 in walnut). By 1974, the Van Eps models had completed the transition to all Baldwin features. The most predominant changes were that all metal parts were now chrome plated, the nameplate was absent, standby switch removed, Baldwin scalloped pickguard and plastic control knobs were now used and a Burns' gearbox truss rod adjustment completed the look of the 7580 and 7581. The original list price was $675, but was discontinued in 1978.

In 1967, Bucky Pizzarelli heard George Van Eps performing in a New York City club and was hooked—Bucky has been an ambassador for the instrument ever since. In a recent conversation Bucky related his feelings about the instrument:

Bucky Pizzarelli

"The 7-string guitar is the instrument of the future. I predict that every guitarist of any importance will be playing a 7-string in the next five years— no matter what style they're into." Bucky is still an extremely active musician. He is featured internationally in festivals and clubs, and sporadically tours with the great French jazz violinist Stephane Grappelli.

In 1989 Howard Alden hooked up with Van Eps to record the album *Hand Crafted Swing*. Howard contends that recording with this jazz sage is what brought him to the epiphany of the seven string. "Sitting next to George and seeing what he was doing, watching his fingers and hearing the voicings, really made it sink in. The 7-string lets me express myself harmonically in a manner that I was always searching for. George Van Eps' term 'Lap Piano' really fits." Howard now plays three handcrafted Benedetto beauties and exclusively plays the 7-string. Howard and George have released three albums together with the most recent being a 1996

Howard Alden

release *Keepin Time* on the Concord label. The influence and stories about George goes on and on. Even though George Van Eps is virtually unknown to the masses, he is truly a legend in the annals of Guitar History.

For the guitarists interested in this instrument they usually had to seek out luthiers who would build or modify guitars for them. Fred Fried, another student of Van Eps, originally had guitar maker Ken Parker (inventor of the Parker Fly) hand-craft a 7-string neck and then installed it on his Gibson 175— Ken called it a Gisben. Fred still has this instrument, but his main axe is now a flat-top acoustic 7-string built by a New Jersey luthier, Mark Wescott. Fred states: "The sound is such that you get spoiled very quickly and as far as the voicings, well, the more you look, the more you find."

Fred Fried

Another 7-string innovator was Lenny Breau. Not unlike his playing, Lenny's instrument was very unusual. It was a nylon string classical style guitar with the 7th string on the high end. Lenny tuned his 7th string to a high A which made any commer-

cially available string too heavy to take the string tension. Necessity being the mother of invention, Lenny cut a few feet of nylon fishing line off a spool and miraculously it sounded great. One spool is said to have lasted him until his untimely death.

Lenny Breau with Charles Chapman – 1976

The most prolific and well-known 7-string luthier is Bob Benedetto. Of his 400 archtops, almost 70 are 7-stringers and this unique guitar now accounts for approximately 25% of his orders. Benedetto is highly regarded for refining the 7-string guitar as evidenced by the jazz luminaries who play them, including: Bucky Pizzarelli, John Pizzarelli, Ron Eschete, Howard Alden and Jimmy Bruno. Bob states: "The 7-String model is part of the guitar's evolution—a very real part. It's perfectly natural to have the additional string; it's not a gimmick. If given the choice, I would only make that model. Once you get involved with it, you realize the possibilities and don't want to go back to just six strings. In short, the 7-String is flourishing and here to stay."

Bob Benedetto

Photo by Donna Chapman

Jazz players are not the only ones that are coming out the closet with their 7-stringers. Luthier Bill

Photo by Donna Chapman

Bill Conklin with Charles Chapman

Conklin, known for his innovative instruments has built scores of custom 7-string guitars for mainly rock and fusion players. His most celebrated was built for Steve Vai while he was touring with Whitesnake. The body was a 3-D carving of two white cobra snakes facing off for battle. It had gemstones for eyes, fossil ivory for the fangs and coral tongues. The entire fingerboard was inlaid with fossil ivory hieroglyphics. Bill claims: "As a luthier, my personal feelings are that the 7-string could be for everyone, but the players in the 6-string market would have to be educated in the use and versatility of the low string. Once more of these cats find out what they can do with that low string... Look Out!"

In 1990 Ibanez introduced the Universe 7-string models which Steve Vai endorsed and helped design. These were the same basic specs as the Jem Series except they used a 48mm neck with seven strings, a low pro edge and an added low B string. The pickups were Dimarzio Blaze humbuckers. In 1992 Ibanez made a limited amount of the S-Series 7-string guitars, too (model 540S7 was only featured in their 1992 catalog). The guitar did not take off like they had hoped and according to Paul Specht of Ibanez, they discontinued production because of limited interest and bridge availability.

A year later, Dream Theater guitarist John Petrucci renewed interest by using the 7-string guitar in the album *Images and Words*. More recently, bands like Korn and Fear Factory have also brought attention to this instrument as well. These bands do not utilize the instrument to the degree that Vai did, but mostly employed it for that low end rhythm crunch. But their success has led Ibanez an entire line of new 7-stringers. Leading the pack is the reintroduction of the Steve Vai Universe 7-string (UV77BK, #3,000), sporting a mirror pickguard, pyramid graphic on the body, and hum/single/hum pickup configuration. More budget conscious players will check out the RG7620 ($1,300), which has DiMarzio 7-string humbuckers, a 5-way pickup-switching system, Lo-Pro Edge double-locking tremolo, basswood body , and a 24 fret-fret maple neck with rosewood fingerboard. But that's not all of the new 7-strings. Ibanez has also produced the AF 207 jazz archtop hollow-body ($3,000) and Artwood Jumbo acoustic ($1,100) which comes with a Fishman Matrix piezo-pickup system. And don't forget about Schecter: They're also producing a cool limited-edition 7-string, with Seymour Duncan pickups, and prices starting at $2,395.

Steve Vai

Summing up, Steve Vai states: "Generally speaking, I like a lot of bottom end. That's one reason why I developed the 7-string guitar. If you're interested in playing classical electric guitar, you can use the 7th string for utilizing counterpoint lines. If you are into jazz, the 7th string will give you the ability to do walking bass lines and chord solo pieces that are totally impossible on a 6-string. If you are into playing Rock and Roll, well just crank it up and start pumpin."

There are many fine luthiers and companies who have built 7-string guitars in the past and are continuing to tool up for the future. The question is: Is this the natural evolution of the guitar or is it the Edsel of this decade?

Charles Chapman

Charles Chapman is a Professor in the Guitar Department at Berklee College of Music where he has taught since 1972. He is a versatile jazz guitarist with extensive performing and recording experience. Charles has been a featured soloist at the NAMM shows since 1997 and continues to perform at guitar shows and music industry conventions internationally. He has performed in concert with, Jerry Jemmott, Carol Kaye, Jimmy Bruno, Howard Alden, Vic Juris and Kenny Burrel to name a few.

He released a jazz duet album with bassist Rich Appleman in 1996, *In Black and White* on DC Records. He performed four tunes on Mel Bay's compilation CD *Master Anthology of Jazz Guitar Solos, Volume One* (formerly *Jazz 2000*) and all nine solos on the CD that accompanies the text *George Van Eps/Guitar Solos* (Mel Bay Publications, Inc.). Charles has recently published numerous texts with Mel Bay Publications, Inc.: *Drop-2 Concept for Guitar, Finger Gymnastics, Making the Changes* and *Bass Line Basics for Guitar*.

As a music journalist he is a frequent contributor to *Guitar Player, Guitar Shop, Acoustic Guitar, Downbeat,* Mel Bay's *Guitar Sessions*® and *Just Jazz Guitar* magazines.

Charles is an Artist Endorser for Fender/Guild Corporation, Benedetto Guitars and Double Treble custom guitar straps.

Other products by Charles Chapman

Bass Line Basics for Guitar (98387BCD) book/CD set

Drop-2 Concept for Guitar (98181) book

Finger Gymnastics (98751BCD) book/CD set

Making the Changes (99069BCD) book/CD set

George Van Eps/Guitar Solos (94822BCD) book/CD set